In the name of Jesus, the Master Storyteller,
we pray, Give us eyes to see the beauty in life;
give us ears to hear its melody;
give us hearts to understand and interpret life to others;
teach us to choose our stories so wisely
and to tell them so well that the story will be remembered
long after the storyteller is forgotten.
Amen.

PRAYER OF THE NATIONAL STORY LEAGUE

REMEMBER the TIME...?

The Power & Promise of Family Storytelling

EILEEN SILVA KINDIG

InterVarsity Press
Downers Grove, Illinois

InterVarsity Press® is the book-publishing division of InterVarsity Christian Fellowship®, a
student movement active on campus at hundreds of universities, colleges and schools of
nursing in the United States of America, and a member movement of the International
Fellowship of Evangelical Students. For information about local and regional activities, write
Public Relations Dept., InterVarsity Christian Fellowship, 6400 Schroeder Rd., P.O. Box 7895,
Madison, WI 53707-7895.

Scripture quotations, unless otherwise noted, are from the Revised Standard Version of the
Bible, copyright © 1946, 1952, 1971 by the Division of Christian Education of the National
Council of the Churches of Christ in the USA. Used by permission. All rights reserved.

Prayer of the National Story League used by permission of the National Story League, 901
Ilyak Place, Fox Island, WA 98333.

Cover illustration: Roberta Polfus

ISBN 0-8308-1965-7

Printed in the United States of America ∞

Library of Congress Cataloging-in-Publication Data

Kindig, Eileen Silva.
    Remember the time—?: the power and promise of family
storytelling/Eileen Silva Kindig.
      p.   cm.
    Includes bibliographical references (p.).
    ISBN 0-8308-1965-7 (alk. paper)
    1. Family—Folklore.   2. Family—United States—Folklore.
3. Storytelling—United States.   4. Family recreation—United
States.   I. Title.
GR465.K56   1997
398.27—dc21   97-12921
                                               CIP

19	18	17	16	15	14	13	12	11	10	9	8	7	6	5	4	3	2	1
12	11	10	09	08	07	06	05	04	03	02	01	00	99	98	97			

For Moira,
my eternal dreamer

Acknowledgments

As this book, and this story, come to their inevitable conclusion, I find myself wishing I were back at the beginning. The opportunity to be richly fed with the stories of so many lives is like dining at the banquet of kings. But rather than leaving me sated, it has only served to whet my appetite for still more stories! To express my gratitude to all the marvelous storytellers who delighted, moved, tantalized and trusted me seems woefully inadequate, and yet, of course, I must try. Without them there would have been no book.

I am also deeply grateful to my family—my husband, Eric, who boiled many a pot of pasta while I labored at the computer; my daughter Moira, a fellow writer who shared the joys and the frustrations of trying to turn passion into prose; and my daughter Caitie, who throughout this year's sojourn has kept me honest and has made me laugh despite the many times she wished her mother were "a house mother" instead of a writer. And then, of course, there's Jessica—my "friend of the right hand"—whose quirky humor reminded me in moments of despair to pull myself up by my pantyhose and get on with it!

I thank, too, my dear friends in my weekly writers' group—Laurie Knowleton, Dandi Mackall and Nancy Peacock—for their encouragement and expectations. They demanded the best from me and would not rest until they got it! A great big thank-you also goes to Betsy Newenhuyse, Don Davis, Cindy Guthrie, Elaine Wynne, Laura Oliver,

Diana Budney, Pat Stropko-O'Leary, Pattilou Judge and the members of the Akron Story League.

Finally, I want to thank my editor, Rodney Clapp, for allowing me the space and the privilege to fly solo on this one, and my agent, Jimmy Vines, who thinks I'm "a real writer." I couldn't ask for more.

One

Outpowering
the Power Rangers

The Power
of Family Stories

I T IS SUNDAY NIGHT, AND MY KIDS ARE WILLINGLY BEING HELD CAPTIVE IN the most undcrused room in America. *What's right with this picture?* Normally, once the candles burn low and the lasagna has been polished off, they're outta here. Like Superman, they leap over tall buildings to get to the TV, the VCR, the computer or the SuperNintendo. But tonight we are gathered around the old oak table in our Wedgwood-blue-and-white dining room doing something so huge it almost takes my breath away. We are telling stories.

"Remember the time we went to Florida and Dad got scared on the Back to the Future ride and I didn't?"

"Remember when the cat ran up the Christmas tree?"

"Did I ever tell you about the time Grandpa Kindig took the Boy Scouts camping in a hearse?"

We laugh uproariously, embellish our favorite tales, interrupt each other and argue hotly over details. Though there are only four of us, the room is so crowded that the cast of characters spills out into the foyer and crams the kitchen. The cousins from Columbus converge with the gang from Hawaii, and the Irish contingent stumbles over the Portuguese—all of them mingling with the ghosts of those who went before us. It is one big multicultural, intergenerational, three-dimensional bash. And God is the guest of honor.

Even as I participate in it, I can feel the vast sacredness of this moment. I know that our stories, homely as they seem on the surface, are holy, uniting us as surely as blood and love and history. But there is something more at work here—something I can only sense.

Where two or three are gathered in my name . . .

Unbidden, the ancient words drift across my mind as I launch into a spirited account of an encounter we had with an elderly couple when Caitie was a baby. For a second they surprise me, but I have warmed to my story, so I merely observe them and move on. It isn't until I hit the punch line and my audience whoops with delight that I realize what is happening. Right here, in the midst of this hilarity, we are praying.

Storytelling is a monumental act. In its finest hour it becomes a psalm of praise and thanksgiving for the love and connection of family. No one else can tell your stories. They belong solely and absolutely to you and to those who make up your intimate circle, whether by birth or by choice. The stories you tell bind you close to one another, yet they give you wings to fly out confidently into the larger world. They teach you how the world works and where you belong in it. But most of all, they open the door to that holy and magnificent place where heaven and earth converge and time hangs in sweet suspension, if only for a moment. The storyteller is the repository of cultural information and the transmitter of history, identity and morality. But the storyteller is also the confabulator, the one who endows the ordinary with wonder, mystery and delight.

"We tell stories because we can't help it," says novelist James Carroll. "We tell stories because we love to entertain and hope to edify. We tell stories because they fill the silence death imposes. We tell stories because they save us."[1]

More than likely, most of your stories are less than spectacular, except to those who play a part in them. They are about the time you thought the family dog was gone forever until he suddenly turned up on the back porch, or about the Thanksgiving Mom worked so hard to make dinner à la Martha Stewart and left the turkey sitting in a cold oven. What makes these treasures of remembrance so infinitely precious is the fact that they never happened before and will never happen again in precisely the same way to anyone else—even though people have lost beloved pets and have ruined dinners almost since the dawn of time. The rich paradox of stories is that they open a door to our individual hearts and usher the entire family of humankind inside.

Once upon a time, families gathered round tribal fires in the depth of winter and sat out under the summer stars, filling the night air with their stories. They spoke of things almost too wondrous to comprehend and of events so ordinary they flooded the heart with the warmth of recognition. But as the material culture grew increasingly sophisticated, the old stories began to seem less stirring. Gradually families stopped telling them and gathered round a succession of big square boxes, each one spewing out electronic stories more dazzlingly contrived and more numbingly familiar than the last. Here on the threshold of the twenty-first century, in a world spinning frenetically from one techno thrill to the next, the old stories of family seem almost like relics of a bygone era, a sort of retro-reflex we occasionally indulge in to mark our triumphs and rationalize our deficiencies. The story of how Great-Great-Great Grandfather Ezra walked from Connecticut to Ohio to settle the frontier with a rocking chair strapped to his back may be historically relevant, and the story of Jenny's stint as an angel in the church Christmas pageant may be poignant enough to break your heart. But if they lack high drama, high technology or high times, Hollywood can best them in a heartbeat.

This societal shift away from the communal fire has cost us dearly. It has stretched and pulled the parameters of story so far that only our peak experiences now seem worthy of being recounted. As a result, families sit silently at the dinner table (if they eat together at all), bolt as soon as they have cleaned their plates and hole up for the evening in separate rooms, each absorbing a separate electronic story at the push of a button. It's not that we don't need stories of our peak experiences. How could we not need them when they mark life's most profound transitions and transformations—the day you graduated from college, got your first job, got married, had a baby, went to Nairobi or sold your first painting? Storytelling is an embracing, living thing. If you let it, it will gather up those big events and place them, like shining stars, among all the precious moments, days and years of your life—most of which are made up of such simple stuff as pruning the roses, baking cookies, rocking the baby, playing with the cat and shopping for groceries.

Imagine the bottom of the ocean scattered with clamshells—white and luminescent, some lying on the surface, others partially submerged in the silt. Inside each shell is a pearl. Some are large and impressive. Others are tiny, no bigger than a mere speck. But each derives from the same Source; each is imbued with beauty, value and meaning. Some are easily accessible, while others must be pried loose from the deep. It is no different with sacred stories—the stories that show the presence of God in our daily lives. Whether long or short, funny or sad, right on the surface or tucked away in a secret compartment of the heart, sacred stories sweep away the stones, shove aside the boulders and clear a path through the dense, sometimes confusing thicket of experience. They also rekindle hope, bring us fully into the flow of life and remind us that God is on the journey with us.

Sacred Stories
Before my small epiphany in the dining room while sharing stories with my family over the remains of an Italian dinner, I would have defined sacred stories as Bible stories, stories recounting the lives of the saints or stories of mystical encounters, conversions or miracles. Today I broaden that definition to include any story that affirms and redeems us. Affirmation can be found in a lopsided birthday cake baked from scratch by a husband whose usual idea of a culinary creation is frozen waffles topped with a spritz of whipped cream from a can. So too redemption can be found on the side of an expressway at 11:00 p.m. when a middle-aged woman stops to help someone change a flat tire in the middle of a snowstorm. Affirmation and redemption are found in the extraordinary, but also in the ordinary—in purple mittens and ponytails, in Easter eggs and

quarters from the tooth fairy. It is up to us to seek it, to recognize it when we find it and to treasure it enough to pass it on.

Of course some stories, by their very nature, are enormous. These are the stories of love and birth, of death and discovery. Most of us have little difficulty recognizing them because of the pivotal role they play in our lives. A cosmic story is one that has either changed you forever or grabbed you by the collar and refused to let go. Although some of your cosmic stories may be tough to tell, they also reflect love and heroism. On the other hand, you may have stories that suggest less noble qualities. Because we are human beings who grope and feel our way along the path to divinity, we sometimes do and say appalling things and have appalling things said and done to us. Do these painfully difficult stories qualify as sacred? There are times, I believe, when they do. The stories that reflect the best in us are what affirm us. But it is the tough stories that will redeem us, if we let them.

In writing this book, I interviewed fifty people from all walks of life. A few were professional storytellers, a few more were poets and writers (as well as professional storytellers), but most were people who tell stories only in the context of their daily lives. When I began the interviews, I envisioned myself sitting over endless cups of coffee in family rooms and kitchens listening to people recount the positive value of storytelling in their lives and in the lives of their families. I expected to laugh a lot, marvel a little, maybe even get a lump in my throat once in a while. And I did. But I also learned that storytelling has a dark underbelly that cannot be ignored.

And ignore it is exactly what I wanted to do! After all, I argued with myself, I was writing a book about the joy of storytelling. Why would I want to muddle it up with a lot of extraneous stuff that made it seem otherwise? But the "stuff" kept recurring. Again and again it turned up and refused to go away. In the end, I had no choice but to acknowledge its presence. When I finally took a deep breath and looked it square in the eye, I realized that in order to celebrate the art of storytelling, it is necessary to confront its shadow side. I also realized that my reluctance to deal with material that challenges my premise mirrors our almost universal reluctance to recount life's less than lovely moments. Yet it is only when we meet the tough stories head-on with honesty, compassion and forgiveness that we discover how they too can be instruments of God's healing grace.

In later chapters we will look at stories that impart wisdom and tell us who we are, celebrate both our uniqueness and our similarities, keep alive our culture and traditions, record our history, bring us closer together, honor our elders and delight in our children. We will also take a close look at tough stories. If you are not now a storyteller, you will learn how you can become one. If you have already experienced the magic of sacred storytelling, you will be challenged to keep that magic alive and growing.

All of us hunger, sometimes without knowing it, for a map to live by. Sacred stories provide us with that sense of direction. Whether we have already lost our way or we just want to pause and check our directions, it is good to be able to pull over to the side of the road and trace the lines and roads that lead us home.

Why We Story

Not long ago my friend Laurie, a fellow writer, surprised me with a wonderful gift—a small Pueblo Indian charm called the Storyteller. It is shaped like a seated woman with children hanging on her body like barnacles. The prototype was created in 1964 when artist Helen Cordero crafted the first clay figure of a storyteller to honor the memory of her grandfather, Santiago Quintana, a skillful storyteller of the Cochiti Pueblo of New Mexico.[2] The most delightful thing about this tiny treasure is something I did not notice at first glance. One of the children lies on her lap with his head at her knees and his feet against her belly, looking raptly up into her face as though all the wonders of the universe hang in her words. The posture is so comical, yet so ardent and whimsical, that it never fails to make me laugh. Eventually I will probably make a necklace of it, but for now, the charm sits on my desk as a reminder that our very survival depends on our stories.

If it seems overly dramatic to link survival with stories, consider for a moment a world without the stories about Jesus. No miracle of the loaves and fishes. No wedding feast of Cana. No nativity, no death and no resurrection. Imagine too that you know nothing of the ancient Greeks or of the experiences of the American slaves or of the

Holocaust survivors. You have never even heard the story of how Grandpa left County Mayo to escape the potato famine and almost died in steerage or how Great-Aunt Sophie only had one payment left to make on her house and lost it to a con artist during the Depression. All you know is what you have experienced in your own life.

Never having heard any of these stories, how do you know who you are, where you came from or what price was paid for your freedom? How do you know that life is not static? What reassures you that good times inevitably follow hard ones? How do you know that life can be better than it is at this moment? Or worse? How do you learn hope and gratitude? How do you recognize danger? And most importantly, where is the promise of salvation and eternal life? With no one ahead of you to shine a light on the path, you are left stumbling in the dark alone.

Without stories we would eventually meld into one homogenous society, all the rich color and diversity of our culture and religion bleached white as bones. The strength of any group of people lies in its belief system and the unique expressions of its most cherished ideals through its art, cuisine, rites of passage, worship and written and oral tradition. Stories are the heart and soul of our culture. They are also the heart and soul of our families. We can sing our stories, act them out, write them, paint them, dance them, draw them, even cook them. But first we must be passionate about preserving them.

Sometimes in telling your stories you will meet with resistance. Adolescents, especially, will shrug them off, appear not to be listening or roll their eyes and sigh, "Oh Mo-o-o-m!" But you have to tell them anyway! For years my older daughter would catch the eye of her amused father, look heavenward and moan, "Here we go again!" whenever I launched into a time-honored tale. Eventually, though, the "here we go again" became part of the storytelling ritual. I expected it, waited for it like a cue, and would almost have been disappointed if it had not been forthcoming. Today she not only knows the stories well but is studying to become a writer, a historian, a teacher—a teller of stories.

Don Davis, a retired Methodist minister, professional storyteller and author from Oracoke Island, North Carolina, has a theory about why teenagers are not typically tuned into storytelling. "Storytelling is an identity-maintenance function," he says. "When the focus is on fortune seeking, nobody tells stories. Adolescents, especially college students, don't want to tell about where they came from because they all came from the stupidest place!"[3]

As parents, grandparents, aunts, uncles and cousins, we are called to be the story keepers *for* them. It is up to us to gather our family stories like ripe fruit, tell them over and over again (whether our audience thinks they are silly or stupendous) and stubbornly refuse to surrender them until we know they have made the transition to the next generation of safe keepers. It is a huge job (figure on it taking a lifetime), but eventually, if we do it well, the fortune seekers will grow older and wiser about the importance of identity maintenance. But first we have to get their attention.

The Electronic Explosion
Sometimes, usually just before it is time to begin thinking about dinner, my twelve-year-old daughter will come into my office and flop down on the couch. Even before she asks me if I am ready to wrap up the day's writing, I know what she wants. (And no, it's *not* the opportunity to spend time chatting with me over the salad greens.) True child of the nineties that she is, she wants me off the computer so she can zoom down the information highway herself, along with millions of other Internet users worldwide.

Not long ago, I stood in an electronic miracle mart waiting to see about having the printer for my computer repaired. Alternative rock blared out of hidden speakers so loudly it should have rattled the brains of shoppers like marbles in a glass jar. But people milled about, apparently unperturbed, comparing prices for items that didn't even exist in my childhood—Pentium processors, videocassette players, compact disc players, laser printers, electronic game systems and stereophonic TVs with screens the size of billboards. In one terrifying second I realized that virtually *every single item* in the store posed a possible threat to our oral tradition.

Last week my local newspaper ran a feature story about the latest rage in self-help groups—twelve-step programs for the Internet addicted. That same week the *Washington Post* reported that support groups such as the University of Maryland's Caught in the Web are forming on college campuses to help students who linger in chat rooms and at game sites so long that they have neither the time nor the energy to hit the books. Excessive surfing has become such a big problem on college campuses that some schools, including the Massachusetts Institute of Technology, have implemented voluntary programs that allow students to request that the university deny them access whenever they try to log on. Other schools are imposing mandatory time limits, while still others are considering flashing a warning on the screen when the amount of time on-line becomes excessive. According to a study conducted by the faculty of New York's Alfred University, nearly half the freshmen who quit school last semester had been pulling all-nighters on the Net. With 75,700 web sites available as of January 1996, and more being added daily, is it any wonder?[4]

The same week I read about the twelve-step groups, a friend told me that she has broken off a relationship with a man she loves because he puts more energy into his electronic relationships than his personal ones. Like so many Net surfers, he has discovered that Internet relationships offer fun and excitement without commitment, repetition or responsibility. I am reminded of what my husband likes to say facetiously whenever I ask him something very basic, like whether it is possible to get the wallpaper off the family-room walls: "We can do it! We have the technology!" The question then becomes, Can we exploit our technological advances and still preserve our stories?

When I think about satellite dishes, cable-TV shopping and other isolationist activities, I get an uneasy feeling. In the introduction to the book *Homespun: Tales from America's Favorite Storytellers,* Jimmy Neil Smith, founder of the National Storytelling Association, writes, "With America's love affair with radio and television, the death knell was struck. Storytelling was being lost, for we had surrendered our ability to entertain ourselves to the disembodied voice and image of the electronic media."[5]

Smith is right about surrender—take away a modern kid's electronic gadgetry, and she heads for the mall. But I would venture to say that there is more at stake than the loss of our ability to keep ourselves amused. George Gerbner, communications researcher, educator and dean emeritus of the University of Pennsylvania's Annenberg School of Communications, put it best when he called television an "institution of general enculturation" that sets the standards for accepted social beliefs and behavior. "Today, television tells most of the stories to most of the people most of the time," Gerbner says.[6]

And those stories are alarmingly violent. Before completing elementary school, the average American child will witness one hundred thousand acts of violence and eight thousand murders on television, much of it on children's shows. According to the National Coalition on Television Violence, the average children's show includes thirty-two acts of violence per hour.[7] We can blame the media and we can pressure the networks for change. But when we fail to make responsible choices, we surrender our own stories and allow Hollywood to choose what stories it wishes us to hear. Instead of learning our identity, values and mores at the feet of the wise members of our tribe, we absorb them from the Power Rangers, or whoever the superheroes-of-the-second happen to be.

Psychologist Jerome Singer estimates that preschool children today average twenty-one hours of TV a week and grade-schoolers an average of thirty-five. This doesn't even include the hours spent on-line, helmeted in headsets or pushing buttons to make cartoon figures jump, fly and flee their would-be captors. It certainly does not leave much time for sitting around on the porch telling stories, does it? Fortunately, storytelling is a movable feast. You can grab half an hour in the car, steal a few minutes at bedtime and pounce on the nights when everybody is huddled together in a booth at Mickey D's after a soccer game. You can also (dare I say it?) pull the plug once in a while. Even if you choose your electronic stories with the utmost care, passive entertainment cannot help you build a treasure-trove of family stories. To build a rich story life, you need to live life fully and expand your family's experiences. This means involving yourself in the life of community.

Technology is not going to fade away. The electronic explosion will continue to explode, enriching our lives in countless ways and posing threats in countless others. I rather suspect that technology is as much the scapegoat as it is the culprit anyway. The remote control, after all, has a button that turns off as well as on. Ultimately, it is up to us to think about who is telling the electronic stories, *why* they are telling them, and whether or not our lives will be uplifted by listening to them. By and large, the electronic stories are told for profit, often *enormous* profit. If your child happens to be uplifted or enlightened along the way, that's wonderful. But the bottom line remains dollars and cents. This is not to say that none of the creators of these programs care about children. I believe some of them do, as evidenced by the sensitivity and quality of their work, and these people deserve our respect and accolades. However, their artistry and humanity in no way negate the fact that children also need stories told by the people who love and care for them. They need stories told to them by Mom and Dad, Grandma and Grandpa, older brothers and sisters, aunts and uncles—all those people in their lives who care enough to tell them exactly what they need to hear.

If used wisely, technology can enhance your storytelling capabilities. If you are really into the high-tech stuff, you can buy a multimedia family album for your computer (such as Delrina's Echo Lake) that allows you to record your stories, plug in photos, sound effects and video clips, separate the stories into categories, tag them and slip them into the appropriate time frame. But even low-tech types (like me) can use a video camera or a simple tape recorder to make a priceless film of Grandma telling the story of her life in Sicily. You can also allow carefully chosen videos or TV programs to serve as a springboard for diving into personal stories.

My family spent New Year's Eve 1994 in a darkened nine-plex cinema off a major four-lane highway swept away by the splendor of *Little Women*. All the way home in the car, my older daughter, Moira, and I shared our childhood love of the book, where we read it, what it meant to us and how we both identified with the character Jo. Somehow this led to a long-ago vacation in Vermont, which meandered off into Moira's childhood tennis lessons, which veered into a hilarious recollection of how she and her childhood friends had formed a secret club called the Red Rose Detective Agency. Not only did the movie evoke stories from both our shared past and her childhood, but it created a whole new story. Sometime in the future we will look back on the lovely New Year's Eve when we went to see *Little Women,* then came home and ate homemade gingerbread while we watched the ball fall on Times Square.

Though we certainly do not want them crowding out real-life heroes, TV superheroes and their stories can have their place. When Moira was small, she slew imaginary dragons in our suburban backyard, holding the bad guys at bay with cardboard swords and tinfoil shields. She raced her big-wheel like the Dukes of Hazzard and played G.I. Joe with the little boy down the street. Not long ago, for a college writing class, she captured the carefree innocence of those days in an autobiographical sketch so beautiful it made my heart stop. Her childhood may have been invaded by popular culture, but from that sea of animation and action figures arose stories of wide-eyed wonder and imagination that will serve her well when she has children of her own. Psychologist and author James Hillman points out that society tends to separate children from adults. Childhood is the time reserved for imaginative play; adulthood is for responsibility. If my daughter can hang on to the wonder of charging after dragons made of clouds, her stories will bridge the gap.

An interesting adjunct to her love of medieval knights and derring-do is that it later linked her to a *real* hero—the grandfather who died two years before she was born. Last year when she was home from college for winter break, we discovered in a dusty box in the attic a battered little book filled with elaborate hand-written rules for an imaginary game of lords and ladies and knights in shining armor. Grandpa Kindig had invented the game in his youth, assigned the various roles to his friends and then kept a diary of its ongoing adventures. In the pages of a cheap green ledger my daughter met a kindred spirit whose imagination and independence spoke to her powerfully across more than seven decades. As author Madeleine L'Engle wrote in an article about storytelling for *Victoria* magazine, "What makes family stories special isn't high drama, but glimpses of personalities that echo ours."[8]

The Big Revival

The good news is that here on the cusp of the twenty-first century, storytelling is still alive and well and living in America. Not only is it battling bravely alongside the electronic explosion, but it is even experiencing an unmistakable revival. When I asked a spokeswoman for the National Storytelling Association in Jonesborough, Tennessee, what she thought about the state of storytelling in the United States today, she replied, "Honey, it's *huge!*"

Because of its famous storytelling festival that annually draws about ten thousand people to the small town of Jonesborough in the southern Appalachian Mountains, the National Storytelling Association (formerly known as the National Association for the Preservation and Perpetuation of Storytelling) is probably the best-known group of its kind. For more than twenty years, it has worked through its publications and programs to show teachers, librarians, ministers, health-care professionals and others who work with people the amazing possibilities of stories for entertainment, education and healing. The group also publishes the bimonthly *Storytelling Magazine.*

The National Story League, based in Altoona, Pennsylvania, likewise works to make stories accessible, especially to those who desperately need to hear them. Since 1903, its mission has been "to encourage the creation and appreciation of the good and beautiful in life and literature through the art of storytelling." The group's current roster shows fifteen thousand members, many of whom are spread out among 250 local groups nationwide. They tell and record stories (on a volunteer basis) in schools, churches, nursing homes, runaway shelters and hospitals—wherever a story might touch a heart, heal a hurt or open a mind to a possibility.

There is also the National Association of Black Storytellers, the Jewish Storytelling Coalition, the International Order of E.A.R.S. (the meaning of the acronym is a secret known only to members!), the Network of Biblical Storytelling—the list goes on and on. According to a posting of storytelling organizations on the Internet, groups have formed in forty-three states and the District of Columbia. Most importantly, there is *us*—you and I and the countless other ordinary people with families who realize, collectively and instinctively, that stories are not merely nice options to be put off until we have more time, or more money, or until "things aren't so crazy." As Bill Buford wrote in *The New Yorker,* "Implicit in the extraordinary revival of storytelling is the possibility that we need stories—that they are a fundamental unit of knowledge, the foundation of memory, essential to the way we make sense of our lives; the beginning, middle, and end of our personal and collective trajectories."

Storytelling is not a magic panacea for what ails us. To imply that it is would be both glib and simplistic. But the fabric of family life is fraying. If ever there were a time when we needed to reclaim our identity, clarify our values and make the kind of memories with our children that will become sacred stories, it is *now.* If each family picks up a few loose, dangling threads, I believe that together we can weave a strong and beautiful cloth.

Things to Talk About

1. Explore the concept of "sacred stories." Can you recall a time when you experienced the holiness of storytelling?

2. How do you feel about the assertion that we need stories for our survival? Can you think of some examples from your own life that illustrate its truth?

3. Discuss the electronic explosion and how it challenges you to keep alive the storytelling tradition. What are some ways you can use technology to enhance storytelling?

Things to Do Right Now

1. Turn off the electronic explosion for a day and do something your family has never done before. It doesn't have to be impressive or costly—just something fun and/or meaningful. Then take time to share thoughts and feelings.

2. Carefully select a video to watch together. Talk about what you saw and relate it to your own experiences. Don't worry about sticking to a theme—allow the stories to go where they will.

Two

Coming Back to the Fire

Stories & Identity

I T WAS ALMOST 10:00 P.M. AND I WAS FADING FAST. EVEN ON A GOOD DAY I'm not much for meetings, and that night I was too exhausted to even try to concentrate. Drowsing, I filled page after page in my notebook with long, skinny intersecting triangles, wishing I were at home in bed with a fat escapist novel. Then from across the room a woman suddenly said, "My family lives its life by Micah 6:8: 'And what does the Lord require of you but to do justice and to love kindness and to walk humbly with your God.' I got that from both sides of my family. It's always been that way."

Instantly my head snapped up. She was a tall, natural-looking woman in late middle age—articulate, assertive, confident. As soon as we adjourned, I made a beeline for her.

"We're Scotch Presbyterians," she explained, clearly eager to share her background. "I was raised in a Scottish community outside Cumberland, Maryland, in the Allegheny Mountains, a big storytelling community. From the time of the Revolutionary War, the men in my family have faithfully served their country, but not one of them has ever picked up a gun in the line of military duty. We've been clergy, cooks and ordinance workers. My son was in the air force assigned to a reconnaissance unit."

She then told me a story about how she and her husband went to Scotland to a church near Loch Lomond, where many of her ancestors were buried. It was late afternoon when they arrived, and the gate to the churchyard was locked. The complex mechanism of the old lock caught her eye immediately. As she held it in her hands, feeling the weight and solidity of the iron, a shiver of recognition and amazement rippled down her spine—it was an exact replica of the one her grandfather, who had been born in the United States, had made back home in Maryland.

She went on to say that her great-grandfather on her father's side had been a violin maker and that every generation of the family had produced at least one violinist. Recently her daughter had a family instrument dating back to 1742 restored to its original beauty and tone. She also told me that every January 25, just as they had when they were small, her four grown children commemorate Burns's Night in honor of the birthday of the great Scottish poet Robert Burns. Story after story poured out, each one somehow linking her children and grandchildren with what she laughingly called "the ancients."

Heading home on the expressway, I felt so energized by the strength of this family's sense of identity that I could hardly contain it. Here they were, two hundred years away from Scotland, and yet they remained Scots to the core of their being. Not only did they know who they were, where they came from and what they stood for, but there was nothing the least bit vague or wishy-washy about any of it. Even more mind-boggling, they had formed and fed this rock-solid identity through storytelling and ritual. For one ridiculous moment I wanted to shout out the window to the people passing by in their cars, "Don't waste another second—start telling your stories!" It seemed *that* urgent.

Today, almost a full year and many hundreds of family stories later, it seems even *more* urgent. Despite the enormous popularity of Alex Haley's book *Roots* and the accompanying TV miniseries, both of which sent us scurrying in droves to the genealogy records back in

1976,[1] few people know much about their family history beyond the begats. Even fewer can state with any conviction what their family stands for right now, much less what their predecessors held dear even a scant two generations ago. Sam Keen, philosopher and former associate editor of *Psychology Today* magazine, as well as a prolific writer on the subject of storytelling, refers to our society as "a people written on from the outside." We moved away from the tribal fires, Keen says, stopped telling our stories and became like blank slates waiting to be scribbled on by whoever or whatever chanced along.[2]

At worst, this lack of identity makes us vulnerable to depression, addiction, loneliness, promiscuity and feelings of alienation. At best, it leaves us as drifters, wandering aimlessly through the mall, hoping Calvin Klein, Armani, Seiko or Sanyo can fill up the emptiness. Episcopal priest and author Matthew Fox calls the ads that pelt us daily with urgings to buy this perfume or that car in order to find happiness and a sense of self-worth "the primary tales of our civilization"—and he is right. Children who come from homes lacking a firm personal and family identity, homes where Fox's "finely crafted stories about consumerism" are the bedtime stories of choice, are at high risk for involvement with cults, drugs, gangs, teen pregnancy—anything that promises to tell them who they are and provides them with an affiliation and a sense of purpose.

When you don't know who you are, who your people are, where you come from or what is expected of you, it is tough to make good choices. Yet that is exactly what these rudderless kids are expected to do. In effect, they are being asked to wander, alone and blindfolded, through a lightless maze filled with obstacles and dead ends while the adults who might have shone a light on the path stand on the sidelines and keep silent. It isn't until they stumble and fall that their families finally, in the offices of counselors and clergy, begin to tell the stories that might have protected them. In order to grow spiritually and emotionally, each of us needs a healthy sense of personal autonomy and membership in a group that recognizes and respects individual differences, yet clearly delineates the common ties—love, origin, race, ethnicity, purpose and moral expectations—that bind its members together. So strong are these needs that if we do not get them met at home, we seek relief someplace else—even if it means dancing with disaster.

A number of years ago, my husband and I provided foster care through the county for a teenage girl who needed a home until the birth of her baby. In the eight months Willi was with us, I saw in dramatic detail exactly what happens when someone grows up without roots. Aside from an awareness that her family had migrated north from Tennessee, the only stories she knew were about drunken brawls and family squabbles. There were no mothering stories to teach her how to raise a child, no Tennessee mountain lore to allow her to pass on a heritage, no spiritual stories to sustain her and certainly no stories to reflect what kind of child she had been or what expectations her family had. She experienced her first "real" Christmas with us!

This is an extreme example, admittedly, but Willi's initial response to her pregnancy was one that is all too common among teens in search of an identity. "I'm glad I'm havin' a kid," she told me shortly after coming to live with us, "because at least I'll have somebody who belongs to me. When I'm a mother I'll even get to be somethin', ya know what I mean?" Her entire identity hinged on a single biological event. But she was too young to realize the enormity of what it asked of her and too "written upon" by casual sex and the drug culture to be able to give it. The journey back to identity is marked, I am convinced, by stories. Until we gather once again around the tribal fires, telling our own stories and listening to the stories of those who came before us, we will claim no sense of continuity, establish no moral viewpoint, and form none of the deep, meaningful relationships that offer us a foretaste of heaven.

The Story of Me

Every child is born with the need for two essential stories—her birth story and the story of how she got her name. Even small children understand on some level the magnitude of these stories because they ask to have them repeated endlessly. It is the same driving need for personal identity that sends adopted children and families torn apart by death and desertion on lifelong quests for their buried roots. Both of my children are adopted from Korea. The fact that I can never give them even the basics about the day they entered this world is painful to me because I know that my ignorance deprives them of their birthright. All I can do to compensate is tell them stories about the enormous baby shower our church gave us while we were waiting for Caitie to arrive and how we called our congressman pleading for help when Moira's paperwork got tangled up in a bureaucratic snarl in Columbus.

But these stories, detailed and well-meaning though they are, are thin and transparent. They speak only of our love, our yearning, our need, while telling them nothing of themselves or of the impact their arrival had on the world. The real gift is the story of what happened after they were placed in our arms, because it gives them a concrete identity and, just as importantly, illustrates our crucial transition from loving them as "dream babies" who gazed at us solemnly out of fuzzy black-and-white adoption-agency photos to loving them as our real flesh-and-blood daughters. Like most small kids, they both adored "the story of me" and wanted it told often and in painstaking detail.

"You forgot the part about how Daddy kept setting off the metal detector at the airport," Moira would say if I tried to cheat and tell the short version. Caitie, always the more hands-on, would interrupt and tell parts of her story herself. "And I had so much hair that I needed a haircut. And when you took me to the beauty shop, they said I was the youngest customer they ever had," she would say, chortling with satisfaction at the specialness of needing a complete trim at age four months.

Your children's birth stories and name stories are crucial to the process of establishing both their individual and familial identity. What they say in effect is, "There was never a person born exactly like you. You are special and important and wonderful, and we are so glad you are part of us and that we can share with you all the things that make us a family."

But even that is not enough! Children need many, many more stories to tell them who they are, especially the ones that show them where they belong in the cosmos—what it means to be born male or female, African-American, Asian, Irish, Polish, Italian, Christian or

Jewish. It is never enough to just know in an abstract way that they *are* any of these things. They need to feel it, experience it, know in their blood and bones what it means. If their place on the continuum happens to be burdened by illness, handicap or poverty, then they need stories of hope and transcendence to help them deal with that too.

A woman named Polly from southern Ohio talked to me at length about the experience of contracting polio as a child during the epidemic of the 1950s. She was nine at the time, an only child in a poor family. Her mom took in ironing, and her dad worked in the strip mines. Every night after work, her father would show up at the hospital before supper to sit by her bed in the big, frightening children's ward lined with iron beds and tell her stories about a little girl named Polly Pickle.

"Polly Pickle was me, of course, but she was a braver, smarter, funnier, more daring me. She'd go through all these terrible trials and come up a winner every time. The last line of every story was always the same: 'Polly Pickle got herself in a pickle, but she got back out again because . . .' That was my cue to say, 'She was the smartest little gherkin in the jar!'" She laughed. "It's corny, I know, but I was a scared little kid with big, big problems. Without my dad, God love him, and his stories, I don't know how I would have gotten through it."

Yet as much as children need to hear stories told *to* them, they also need to be allowed to tell stories of their own. This will be covered in greater depth in a later chapter, but I mention it now because it impacts the development of personal identity in two significant ways. When a child tells a story about his own experience—at school, at church, at a soccer game or in the neighborhood—he has the opportunity to stand back from both the story and the experience, observe his feelings and actions, and learn how others respond to him. He also gets the chance to experiment with the dual roles of communicator and entertainer. When children realize that their parents think their stories are important, they develop the self-confidence to keep sharing them and thus keep sharing themselves. The etymological root of the word *story* is "to know." To know our children, to help them know us, to know where we have been, who preceded us and where we are headed now, we have no choice but to return to story. Only when we open ourselves to its truth will we find the meaning of our lives.

The Story of Us

Every family story has two basic functions. The first is to illustrate all the glorious, crazy, eccentric, touching, wonderful ways that your family is different from every other family that is now, ever was, or ever will be. The second is to remind you of your spiritual connection with families everywhere, from Topeka to Timbuktu. Although family stories may also serve other valuable purposes simultaneously, sacred stories *always* accomplish these two goals. Any story that fails to do so diminishes both the teller and the audience, alienating them from each other, from God and from their finest selves. With this in mind, let's take a look at some of the ways you can begin to strengthen your family's identity through storytelling.

An obvious starting point is ethnicity. Families who retain even a small measure of their culture of origin can keep it alive in their children by honoring the stories, traditions and rituals of the ancestral home. One young mom I spoke with is two generations away from "the old country," yet she still holds fast to her Bohemian background. She immediately linked family stories with the winter Saturday mornings of her childhood. Waking up to the smell of freshly baked pastry wafting up the stairs, she would lie in bed savoring the warmth, scent and security of the moment. Finally, when the anticipation of hot, fruit-filled kolaches became too deliciously enticing, she would slip out of bed and go down to the warm, steamy kitchen where her mother stood at the kitchen table, elbow deep in an enormous mixing bowl. Judy would sit at the table, munch kolaches and sip tea laced with hot milk, listening as her mother sifted flour and told stories of their Eastern European background. Emigration stories, Depression stories, love stories, funny, sad, triumphant stories—out they rolled along with a yard of buttery dough.

Today Judy juggles a husband and two children, a house and a job as a newspaper columnist, as well as volunteer activities ranging from church to Cub Scouts. To try to fit in a regular Saturday baking day would be like attempting to do the family laundry on a scrubboard. Yet she still manages to dust off the old recipes for holidays and special events, sprinkling the familiar stories like sweet cinnamon throughout her children's days. Because her sense of identity is deeply rooted in stories, Judy knows that storytelling is important work, every bit as crucial as earning a living.

If your family can no longer trace its ethnic roots, you can keep alive its American past by bringing to life the people who preceded you in the United States—even if your knowledge of them only goes back as far as your own parents. A remarkable example of honoring an American heritage is the experience of Barbara Tull, a professor of speech at Ohio Wesleyan University. Not long after an elderly aunt died, she found in a desk drawer a packet of brittle, yellowed letters written by her great-grandmother, Rachel Kerr Johnson. Over the next several years, Barbara pieced together the story fragments she had heard as a child with the astonishingly detailed accounts in the letters. The result was a cohesive tale that sang and danced with such vitality she eventually told it in the book *Affectionately, Rachel: Letters from India, 1860-1884* (Kent State University Press, 1992).

As Barbara shared with me the story of her family's long tradition of service as Presbyterian missionaries in Futtehpore, India, I sat spellbound in the front parlor of her imposing brick Victorian home. Like wisps of cotton candy swirling around a paper cone, the stories spun until I could feel the intense heat, smell the mangoes and see the passing parade of bejeweled elephants that her great-grandparents encountered as they made their home in an exotic land. But most of all, I could feel the emotions of real people who were wrenched with pain at having to leave their children behind in the United States to be educated and were worried about the brothers in Pennsylvania who were caught up in the bloody conflict of the American Civil War. Like a pendulum, her stories swung—back and forth, back and forth—between triumph and heartbreak. By the time she finished, almost three hours had passed. I had to shake myself back into the twentieth century. Now *that's* storytelling!

Barbara's stories are fascinating and are important to an understanding of the American missionary experience. But what they give to her entire extended family and its descendants is something that far exceeds literary or historical merit. These stories gift them with two important pieces of their identity—their proud American past and a Christian faith so bold and unshakable that their predecessors were willing to risk their lives, leave their homes and even part with their children for the privilege of doing God's work. Although the family's long chain of missionaries finally snapped in the twentieth century, the link between the values of the past and those of the present remains unbroken through their involvement with civil rights and peace and justice issues, as well as in their continued commitment to their Presbyterian roots. All five of Barbara's children have studied, worked or conducted research in a foreign country. One is a political affairs officer with the UN peacekeeping project in eastern Croatia, and another worked as an international partner with Habitat for Humanity in Nicaragua, Guatemala, Cambodia and England for four years and is currently studying at Harvard for a graduate degree in international development.[3]

If you are fortunate enough to be able to trace your family's walk of faith, you have real treasure to bestow on your children. But even if you lack a long religious heritage like the Tull family's, you can begin to create one right now by making your beliefs part of your daily life. New stories will pop up like wildflowers from the fertile ground of family prayer, tradition and involvement in activities that express your belief in God and the tenets of your religion. Families share stories of gathering greens to make their own Advent wreath, working together at their church's summer camp, sending care packages to U.S. military troops during the Persian Gulf conflict, traveling with their fellow church members to El Salvador to help build houses for the poor, and simply walking along the ocean celebrating the glory of creation. Whatever you choose to do, no matter how large or how small, these stories send your children a powerful message that says, *We are a people of faith.*

Of course, implied in the message is the expectation that family members will adhere to a certain code of moral behavior. These expectations need to be clearly stated and need to apply to everyone in the family. They also must not be so rigid or so unreasonable that they stifle personal growth. Stories of family heroes whose actions mirror the family's values and beliefs capture the imagination of children and imprint themselves deeply in their minds and hearts, even though it may take years for it to become apparent.

Until my daughter went to college, I did not realize how strongly my own family's stories stress the importance of giving to others. She joined Amnesty International, signed up as a volunteer at an inner-city community center and joined a service club. One evening after she wound up a lengthy, convoluted long-distance story about Christmas shopping for a needy family through the Salvation Army, I asked her if she had any time left to study. "I thought you'd be happy that I'm doing all this stuff," she replied, a tad defensively. "Isn't giving to other people what we're supposed to be about?"

Uh, well, actually it is. Point taken.

If you are not sure what value or ethic strikes the deepest chord in your own family, take a look at the stories you tell again and again. Buried within each one is a clue that will tell you much about the people who influenced you and about the influence your stories may be having on your own children. Look at your favorite family stories collectively. Can you discern a common theme? One woman told me that her family's stories center largely around the Depression and other times of financial struggle. "The point they make about our family is that we may not have much, but we always manage to survive and we don't have to take charity to do it," she said. "It's so strong that even to this day I have trouble asking people for help. I'd rather figure things out myself or make do."

Along with moral and ethical values, family stories contain myriad beliefs and perceptions about life. Some of these, such as whether to approach life with optimism or despair, are so important in the development of identity that they shape the core beliefs that determine how individual members live their lives. When I was growing up, my family tended to view the world as a scary, unpredictable place where disaster lurked in the shadows like a cat burglar, ready to strike us at our most vulnerable moment. As far as I can recall, no one ever overtly stated this, but it was nonetheless the message of nearly every story told over the endless cups of tea we drank sitting around the kitchen table late at night. So deeply did I assimilate my family's beliefs as a child that even logic, faith and experience were not enough to totally shake them off in adulthood. Though I made a conscious decision not to pass these beliefs on to my own kids, the quest for optimism continues to be an ongoing struggle for me. My friends Jessica and Nancy, on the other hand, grew up with stories that reflected a benign view of the world. As a result, they are not prone to excessive worry. Both feel comfortable in a world they expect to bring them good.

It is important to note that it isn't only family stories of obvious significance that speak volumes about deeply cherished ideals and beliefs. Often the ones that seem slight and insignificant serve as more transparent windows to the soul than the ones that loom largest. When asked to analyze his family's stories for attitudes about life, one man thought for a moment and then burst out laughing. "That's easy: buy, don't rent, and always drive a Ford!" he said. But after retelling a few of these stories and mulling them over, he began to see that beneath the humor lay a deep regard for the family home and a pride in the family's perceived ability to recognize quality.

Albert Einstein's My Third Cousin Twice Removed

Sometimes, especially when a family admires a particular personality trait, a certain measure of exaggeration creeps into its stories. A friend commented that her husband's family likes to say, "It takes Grandpa six months to paint a house, but he has such a steady hand that when he's finished you can't see *one single* bobble or brush stroke." Obviously, even the best painter, working on something as big as a house, will produce some minor imperfection. The point of the story is that here is a man of such rare talent, who takes such pride in doing even the most routine tasks, that no amount of time or effort is too much to ask. This family perceives an artist in its midst.

Such embellishments are not usually considered lies. Most families believe them to be true, whether or not there is any factual basis for them. In its search for identity, each family seeks to find the one thing that makes its members more remarkable than "ordinary" people.

This desire for specialness is what drives us to rifle the pages of our family's past for associations with notable people or historical events. Of the fifty people I talked with, more than a third could readily name an illustrious ancestor. While this is hardly a scientific study, I heard claims to celebrities as diverse as Mary Queen of Scots, Dolly Madison, Buffalo Bill Cody, Nathan Hale, Robert E. Lee, Miles Standish, Sophia Loren, Liza Minnelli's father and even Mae West's bodyguard! My own family takes great pride in the fact that my mother's first cousin turned actors into apes for the *Planet of the Apes* movies of the 1960s and was interviewed on the old *Johnny Carson Show*. No matter how nebulous the connection or how iffy the accomplishment, every family has its claim to fame!

Specialness by association is no new phenomenon. When the French historian and political philosopher Alexis de Tocqueville visited the United States in 1835, he wrote, "There is hardly an American to be met who does not claim some remote kindred with the founders of the colonies. As for the scions of the notable families of England, America seemed to me to be covered with them!"[4]

Carving out a unique identity through exaggeration and/or association is fun and can help kids see that "greatness" is within reach. It can also be helpful, especially in regard to historical events such as World War II or the 1970 Kent State tragedy, for families to see themselves in the context of the "bigger picture" rather than as isolated entities. Exaggeration and association become a problem when family members who do not exemplify the desired trait or belief feel alienated and/or diminished. It is also a problem when so much emphasis is placed on being special that families feel superior to others instead of connected to them.

Identity Through Community

Far more important than exotic experiences, bigger-than-life characters and amazing talents and feats are the common threads woven throughout stories told by families in every corner of the world. The fact your family is unique is one of the main things we all have in common! We also share the universal experience of being created by the same God and feeling the same human emotions. From

Bosnia to Biloxi, parents love their children, worry about them and want the best for them. From Vietnam to Vancouver, families share meals, have fun together, participate in rituals, celebrate holidays and mourn their dead. As you begin to see the bigger picture, you begin to realize the universality of emotions and experiences and feel the tug of commonality that opens the heart to empathy and compassion for people whose ways are not your ways. But first you have to leave the family hearth to join the groups gathered around larger fires.

Membership in a community is a key process in forming a strong family identity for three reasons: (1) it enhances feelings of belonging, (2) it provides an opportunity to see your family in a larger context and (3) it allows your family to see itself reflected in the eyes of the community. Church groups, school activities, athletic teams, service organizations, hobbies, clubs, political organizations and the workplace all provide valuable links between families. Some affiliations stand firm for a lifetime, while others change as your family moves through the inevitable stages of growth. But the broader you stretch the horizons and the more diverse people your family comes to know, the more global your sense of community will be.

On Christmas Eve twenty-one years ago, a soft snow fell as eleven people gathered around a candle-lit dining table in a small Ohio town. A passerby looking in through the window might have thought the scene on a Hallmark card had come to life, with the glittering tree in the corner, the golden turkey, and Joan Baez singing "O Holy Night" in French in the background. But the passerby could not possibly guess that only a year before the man and the woman sitting at each end of the table had not known a single one of the shining faces reflected in the glass. For my husband, Eric, and me 1975 was the year that rocked the world. In April, just days after Saigon fell to the North Vietnamese, we met a Trailways bus in Cleveland bearing eight Vietnamese refugees—two parents and six children—whom we had agreed to sponsor. In September, on the day Eric's aunt and uncle were killed in a house fire, we met a plane in Chicago carrying a five-month-old baby from Seoul, South Korea—our daughter, Moira Mi-Ahn.

When I think about that long-ago Christmas Eve night, images tumble over one another like bits of colored glass in a kaleidoscope: the chocolate yule log that Thi, the Vietnamese mother, had made and carefully scripted with the words *Joyeaux Noel* as a gift for us; Moira's little feet in white high-top baby shoes kicking against the wooden high chair with unrestrained glee; the youngest child, Ha-Phong, singing for us in Vietnamese. All we could make out was "Bong, bing, bong! Bong, bing, bong!" and a few heartfelt "Heys!" But "Jingle Bells" remains "Jingle Bells" in any language. What thrills me still is the fact that we came together on that hushed, magical, perfect night from three separate cultures to laugh, celebrate and rejoice in the birth of the Christ child.

We do not have to be a people "written on from the outside." Within ourselves, our culture, heritage, religion and community lie all the wit, wisdom and richness we could ever need to author the stories that will "live, move and have their being" long after we have turned them over to the next generation of story keepers. But first we have to come back to the fire. First we have to draw close and utter again the ancient words, "Once upon a time . . ." And first we have to listen.

Things to Talk About

1. How have the stories you heard as a child impacted your personal identity? Your family's identity? What have you chosen to pass along? Why?

2. Reflect on the characterization of our society as a "people written on from the outside." Who or what do you think is claiming authorship?

Things to Do Right Now

1. Select a Bible verse or a write a statement that reflects your family's identity. Identify and tell the stories that best exemplify it in action.

2. As a family, make a list of all the ways you're currently living out this statement and think of how you might do it even more fully.

3. Choose one recipe, tradition or ritual from your heritage and engage the entire family's participation in recreating it. Tell the stories of those who did it before you (or times when you did it

yourselves if it's something you created), how it came to be, and why it's meaningful. It needn't be ethnic. Be creative!

4. Have a "Story of Me" week. Each evening plan the menu featuring the favorite dishes of a different member of the family. Tell stories that reflect that person's specialness and contribution to the family. Choose stories that show how much the honoree is valued.

Three

Building Cathedrals
Stories & Moral Values

T HREE MEN WERE HARD AT WORK ONE DAY WHEN A PASSERBY STOPPED to ask them what they were doing. "Making a living," replied the first man, sighing heavily.

"Cutting stone," responded the second, efficiently maneuvering his chisel.

The third man put down his tools and gazed heavenward. "Building a cathedral," he said.

I love that story. Every time I tell it, however, I have to fight an overwhelming compulsion to explain it. It is bad enough when I am talking to adults, but get me anywhere near my kids and—*wham!*—I want to tack on a moral and drive it home with a sledgehammer. I have seen enough rolling eyeballs, grimacing faces and tuned-out stares over the years to know that there is nothing that can ruin a great message (not to mention a great story) faster than moralizing. Yet nine times out of ten I still fight the tendency to go for the cheap shot, even though I know that a good story is perfectly capable of standing on its own two feet.

Almost every parent has had the experience of seeing a morality tale fall flatter than the Dow Jones average on Black Monday. Intuitively we know that if storytelling can help us build a strong sense of personal and family identity, it can also instill solid values. That is because identity and character are so entwined that it is almost impossible to work on one without influencing the other. Instead of storming in like commandos peppering our kids with sermons, we would do well to follow the example of the master Storyteller. With infinite wisdom, Jesus planted his parables like seeds in the minds of his disciples and allowed them to bear fruit in their own time. It may have frustrated them and even made them a little crazy at times, but Jesus knew that the best lessons are always the ones we figure out for ourselves.

Using family stories to teach kids values is a wonderful way to shine up the family heroes, personalize abstract virtues like honesty and courage, and even bridge the gap between the generations. The right story told at the right moment can open a mind to a new way of thinking and can turn a heart away from darkness, especially when the story, not the parent, makes the point. Charles A. Smith, a psychologist specializing in adult-child relationships, says, "Children learn from stories. If actions speak louder than words, then stories speak louder than lectures."[1] Sometimes, however, our emotions can get in the way of the process.

Greg, a father of four, struggles fiercely to raise his kids to be thankful for what they have and to appreciate even the smallest blessings. Greg grew up as one of nine kids. Money was so tight in his stern, joyless family that he was twenty years old and on his own before he ever ate a meal in a restaurant. Today, as president of a medium-sized furniture manufacturing company, he can give his own family a comfortable standard of living. But sometimes it seems to him that his three kids just don't appreciate it. "A perfect example was last spring break when we went to Disney World," he lamented. "We stayed at the best hotel—did it all, saw it all, had the best time ever. But no sooner had we arrived home than they started grousing because we hadn't gone to Universal Studios."

Greg says that he furiously countered this barrage of complaints by pulling out a story about the time he won two Cleveland Browns tickets in a sixth-grade essay contest, but never got to use them because his parents flatly told him they had neither the money nor the time to make a thirty-mile trip for something as frivolous as a football game. "Now *that's* deprivation!" he concluded, slamming his hand on the table to hammer home the point. "You guys don't know how lucky you are."

The story failed miserably.

"I ended up lecturing them about how they never appreciate *anything*, which isn't even true," he admitted. "Many times they thank me for what I do for them, but by then I was on a roll. I told them every hard-luck story I had. And the more I talked, the madder I got. Later I realized that it wasn't even about them anymore. It was about me and how deprived *I'd* felt."

It takes a lot of wisdom to realize that revisiting tough stories can resurrect strong, unresolved feelings. Greg's instinct to tell his kids a story from his own childhood to help them learn to be more thankful was a good one, except for one thing—the unresolved pain of the past overshadowed what was happening in the present. Before you can effectively tell a tough story to make a point, you have to be sure you can remain focused on the issue without launching off into a diatribe.

Compare Greg's experience using storytelling to teach his children values with that of Christine, the mother of a grown son and a fourteen-year-old daughter, Ashley. When Ashley was in the fourth grade, the family was preparing its annual holiday box for a family in the community that could not afford a Christmas celebration. Even as a preschooler, Ashley had enjoyed making her own personal contribution. Just the year before she helped clean the basement to earn enough money to buy three packages of name-brand chocolate pudding ("the kind Bill Cosby eats") and had wrapped each one individually with a scrap of candy cane paper, two yards of sticky tape and enough curling ribbon to tie up Cleveland. But that Christmas she was resentful at having to break into her piggy bank. "If these people weren't so lazy, they'd get a job and then they wouldn't even need this stuff," she complained, repeating a sentiment she had overheard in the church vestibule the week before.

At that, Christine's blood pressure threatened to soar off the charts. Ever since they had moved to their small town in New Jersey, the church's Christmas dinner program had been dearer to her heart than any other volunteer activity. The thought that her own child would balk at making a contribution was enough to make her want to "spit nails." But instead of flying into a fit of moral indignation, she took her aggression out on the carrots she was chopping for stew, took a deep breath, counted to ten . . . and told a story.

"You know, Ashley," she said calmly, "every time I think of Christmas boxes it reminds me of the Christmas I was ten. It was 1959, and as you know, I lived with my grandmother—your great-grandmother—in the old house on Sherman Street. It was so cold that December that even our dog Chippie's breath froze. One morning when Grandma went out to the doghouse in the backyard to feed him, she found a perfect icicle *arf* lying right there on top of the snow! Our house didn't have any heat upstairs, so I think a few words probably froze up there too. If I'm not mistaken, they were *happy* and *excited*, because that's what we were as we snuggled under the quilt in her lumpy old bed and planned our surprise for the box my Sunday-school class was putting together for a needy family."

Christine is the kind of storyteller people listen to even when they don't want to—and Ashley was certainly in no mood to listen to some goody-goody story about Christian charity back in "the olden days." But the part about the frozen *arf* made her laugh, and before she knew it she was hooked.

"Now Grandma didn't have much money—just her social security check every month," Christine continued. "But she was so generous that Uncle Marty always used to say she was the kind of woman who'd give her only coat to a tailor if one asked her for it. She also happened to bake the best clove cake in town."

"I know that cake!" Ashley cried. "It's the high, spicy one you always make on Christmas Eve."

"Right," her mom said. "So you know how pretty it is all covered with powdered sugar. But it's very, very expensive to make. It takes almost a whole box of raisins, four different spices, and chopped walnuts, not to mention five eggs and a cup of buttermilk. But we figured that if I shoveled a few sidewalks and Grandma cut back at the meat market, we could afford to make one for the box."

Ashley rolled her eyes at the idea of having to sacrifice to make something as ordinary as a dessert, but Christine resisted the urge to spin off into a lecture about the realities of life in the inner city and concentrated on how thrilled she was to walk into Sunday school carrying the enormous clove cake. When the class crowded around to admire its lacy top, she told them how she had held a paper doily in place while her grandmother sprinkled the soft white sugar through the holes.

"On Christmas Eve," she continued, "Grandma and I were having supper before we walked up to the church for the candlelight service when we heard a car pull into the driveway. 'I wonder who that could be at this hour,' Grandma said. She got up and snapped on the porch light, and there stood Mr. McKinnon from the church vestry. The porch kind of sagged so he was standing on an angle, but we tilted our heads to the right and saw that he was holding a great big cardboard box. Guess what was perched on top."

"I don't know. What?"

"A great big clove cake with a lacy sugar top!"

"You mean the basket was for *you?*" Ashley gasped, clearly amazed by the tale's O. Henry ending.

Christine nodded and concentrated on her chopping. Several hours later Ashley came over and sat beside her on the couch. "Mom," she said, resting her head on Christine's shoulder, "do you think maybe we could buy all the stuff and make a clove cake for the family we're sponsoring? It might be sorta neat. I could for sure buy the raisins with my own money. And maybe even the walnuts too."

Unlike Greg's story of an underprivileged childhood, Christine's account of growing up poor hit the bull's-eye. She did not allow negative emotions from the past to creep into the narrative. She kept her anger in check, lightened the moral with a touch of humor and let the story stand or fall on its own merit. Without realizing it, she followed every rule of successfully telling a family story to point out a moral truth! Of course, there will be times when humor is not appropriate to the story you need to tell, but when it is, it can be a highly effective tool in setting a receptive tone and dissipating tension. Anytime you can make a kid laugh, you have won his attention.

Shining Up the Family Heroes

Obviously Christine's story was a success, because it brought about the desired behavior almost immediately. But if you look a little deeper, it becomes clear that what is far more gratifying than Ashley's change of action is her change of *attitude.* By engaging her emotions with a funny, bittersweet story she will never forget, her mother did two critical things—she gave "the poor" a very real, lasting identity and cast family members as role models, thereby setting the stage for the formation of family heroes. Before a child can embrace the values, attitudes and actions of such dramatic heroes as Mother Teresa or Martin Luther King, he has to know what it even means to *be* a hero. What better way to learn than over the kitchen counter watching your mom cook dinner?

The word *hero* seems to have fallen out of favor these days. Or maybe it is just that we have confused it with that other word—*celebrity.* Given a good public relations agent, almost anybody can be a celebrity, but genuine heroes are a rarer breed of bird. For a long time now, we have given so much press to the public icons who dazzle us with outrageousness, that many, if not most, kids fail to grasp the concept of a hero as someone who embodies our society's highest aspirations, beliefs and ideals. Ten years ago, a college president was quoted in the *New York Times* as saying, "I think students need heroes—period. But when I meet with students again and again and ask them who their heroes are, the question strikes them as being odd."

On February 14, 1996, the TV show *Prime Time Live* aired a sobering segment about children and moral values. Interviewers asked a group of middle-class American parents whether they felt they had been successful in transmitting moral values to their children. All of them felt confident that they had. But as soon as the parents were out of earshot, the kids turned this assumption topsy-turvy with enough candor to make you weep with despair. Seventy percent said they knew that adults lie and cheat to get what they want, and they saw no reason why they should not do the same. Even more astounding was their answer to the question "Who are your heroes?" Although African-American children were more likely to be able to name names, the vast majority said they had none— *including family heroes.* A few even went so far as to say they did not feel they needed anything to aspire to! These were not gang members, druggies or throw-away kids. They were the boy your daughter could grow up to marry and the girl who might wind up sharing a lab table with your son in medical school someday.[2]

Ernest Becker, a Pulitzer Prize-winning author who made significant contributions to the field of psychoanalysis before he died in the 1970s, once wrote to his eminent colleague the late Rollo May, "Society has to contrive some way to allow its citizens to feel heroic. This is one of the great challenges of the twentieth century." I would venture to say that it is going to be one of the great challenges of the twenty-first century too—and one we had better take up with a white-hot fervor. Unless kids can discover at the family fire the role models they need to create both a strong character and a loving heart, they will have little impetus to look for heroes in the "real" world and little ability to recognize them when they see them.[3]

Family heroes do not need to be bigger than life. They do not even need to be perfect. Perfection has less to do with heroism than it does with myth. God did not create perfect creatures and call them human beings. God created human beings and deemed them capable of heroic behavior. I have heard enough heartwarming stories about family heroes to believe that most of us have at least one of them nesting in the family tree, or, at the very least, one person who was a hero once in his life.

From the time they were very small, my children have heard me tell the story of my second date with the man who became my husband. It was January 1970. A blizzard raged as we picked our way across the icy parking lot toward a trendy, upscale restaurant. I was wearing high heels and a cocktail dress; Eric, a suit and new dress shoes with slippery soles. Suddenly a car got stuck in a snowdrift. The driver gunned the engine repeatedly, but the car stubbornly refused to budge. Though at least a dozen people passed by, few even glanced at the mishap, much less offered to help. The temperature hovered somewhere below zero, and Eric had left his topcoat in the car, but he did not hesitate. He pushed and rocked and pushed some more until the car was back out on the road, fishtailing its way down West Market Street through the blinding snow. As I stood in the blue-lit doorway of the restaurant watching him, my heart leaped. *This is the man I'm going to marry,* I thought. Many, many times I have heard our daughter Moira comment that she intends to marry a man just like her dad.

Heroes come in many guises. Some crack their gum, wear mismatched socks, do not exercise enough and look like unmade beds. Others cannot pass a mirror without checking their hair, wear only designer labels, drive badly and refuse to eat anything that comes out of a can. What they have in common is the fact that for one shining, golden moment they reached so high that their toes actually left the ground, and they flew. The hero of your story could even be you. There is nothing wrong with sharing your moral victories as long as you share your moral struggles too. There is also nothing wrong with telling stories of moral outrage when you encounter forces in the world so cold they glaze your soul with frost.

A woman named Jessica lives in a big, mustard-yellow house with her husband, three kids and three cats. One day she came home and told her family a devastating story. She had taken her eighty-six-year-old father to the doctor for a checkup after his latest round of chemotherapy. After the exam the doctor began to talk to her as though her father had faded quietly into the tasteful navy-blue-and-cream striped wallpaper. Although he listened carefully, her dad did not offer any comment because he was too busy fumbling with the tiny buttons and squinting to see the buttonholes in the dark green fabric of his sport shirt. Jessica knew how hard he was struggling, but also knew that his pride demanded that he dress himself unaided. Finally, when the task was completed, her father looked up and posed a question the average layperson would not have enough knowledge to ask. But the doctor was neither interested nor impressed. "What would you need to know a thing like that for?" he snapped. "You can't even button your own shirt!"

Every time Jessica tells that story, her kids know that she has fire in her eye. They also know that their mom was the hero of the hour. Seeing the missed buttonhole and the look of humiliation on her father's face, she fixed the doctor with a steely stare and said evenly, "Take all the time you need, Dad. We'll run by the library on the way home and you can do your *own* research." Not long ago I watched her nineteen-year-old son, Andy, a "cool" guy with a California tan, patiently help an elderly guest up their long gravel driveway for a graduation party. I couldn't help but think of that story.

Another parent who became the hero of his own story is Jim, the father of a third-grader. When his son was caught cheating on a spelling test, Jim shared the account of how he too had once panicked during a test and had looked at someone else's paper. The teacher did not seem to notice, but after the test was finished, she walked over, picked up both his paper and his seat mate's, ripped them in half and said calmly, "I think you know why that happened." Without saying another word, she strode to the front of the class and resumed the lesson, leaving Jim slumped at his desk in misery.

Retelling the thirty-year-old story brought back a flood of feelings—mortification at having been singled out in front of the class, guilt at having cost his friend a passing grade and shame that he had done something he knew was wrong. Jim did not hold any of it back. He told his son exactly what that experience was like and how it made him realize that no grade, no gold star and no teacher's praise could ever cause him to compromise his values, self-esteem and friendships. "It was a great moment," Jim said, recalling it. "Instead of flying off the handle, I told my boy that I understood what it was like to make a mistake because I'd made them myself. It was amazing the way that little story reached him. We were no longer adversaries, but two guys who shared a common struggle and learned a valuable thing."

Stories by Osmosis

Although storytelling can be used effectively to teach kids morals, more often they pick up values by overhearing stories their parents tell others, by absorbing stories that they are not actively paying attention to or that seem almost too commonplace to be worth remembering. Judy, the young mother who told me the story about watching her mother make kolaches, realized this in an especially poignant way when her young son, Jaimie, shared something that had happened at school that day. "Mom, I'm worried about Toby," he said suddenly as they were waiting in traffic for a red light to change on the way to a Cub Scout meeting.

"Oh? Why's that?" she asked, smiling to herself. The two boys were best friends, but sometimes had differences of opinion over such weighty matters as which Star Trek movie was the best and whether they should choose cheese popcorn or chocolate chip cookies for a snack.

"He doesn't know the difference between a want and a need."

Startled, Judy did not notice the light turn green. After a few seconds of probing, she discovered that the teacher had asked the class to make two columns and label one "Needs" and the other "Wants." Toby had written SuperNintendo under "Needs."

"How do you know that's not a need?" she asked her son as the car behind them honked loudly.

Sighing deeply with all the beleaguered patience of a very weary seven-year-old, he replied, "Because of the stories, of course."

"The stories" turned out to be the simple anecdotes Judy tells almost reflexively. Some of them are so tiny that they span no more time than it took you to read this sentence. An image flashed into my mind of bright green peas falling *ping!* into the bottom of a metal dishpan while rain drummed a steady counterpoint on a metal roof. Several years ago, Judy told me a story about sitting on the front porch shelling peas with her mother during a thunderstorm and being flooded by a strange, unexplainable joy. Countless times since, I have stood at my own front door watching a summer shower and thought of that small, exquisite moment. How amazing and how miraculous that a child had heard it too and had known without being told how deeply it spoke to the needs of the spirit.

Another mother shared a similarly enlightening story of how stories can teach children by osmosis. As she and her husband and young daughter were visiting her in-laws one evening, her father-in-law began telling a racially bigoted story. Both Marie and her husband, Ed, tried to suggest that it might not be an appropriate story to tell in front of their child, but Ed's dad brushed aside their objections like so much clutter. Then four-year-old Lindsey looked up from her coloring book and said, "You shouldn't say that word, Poppa. It's not nice and it hurts people's feelings." Only the day before, when it had seemed she was engrossed in *Sesame Street* on TV, she had overheard her father recounting an incident at work. Nobody had to spell out for her the fact that her dad did not like to hear people called ugly racist names—the story had said it all.

Do not be surprised if your kids shrug off an important family story the first time they hear it. Even if they do take it in and seem to appreciate it, they may not understand its full significance until later. Very often we have to hear a story over and over at many different stages in our lives before we begin to understand the subtle (and sometimes not so subtle) nuances. Story refuses to be rushed. It reveals its layers of meaning only as we become spiritually and emotionally ready to assimilate them.

Anne, a middle-aged woman from New York, shared with me a story she heard repeated throughout her life but did not come to fully comprehend until a few years ago. At the turn of the century her grandmother Lena set sail from Scotland alone, filled with all the wild fear, excitement and longing of an eighteen-year-old girl about to be married. Her fiancé, Thomas, had left their village the previous year to make his fortune in the United States and had finally sent passage for her to join him. When the long, grimy journey at last ended at Ellis Island, Lena's heart sang at the prospect of seeing her beloved Thomas. But instead of Thomas, she was met by a stranger who had come to tell her that her fiancé had contracted hepatitis and was deathly ill. Two days before what should have been their wedding day, he died.

With no money for the return voyage and a family too poor to send her any, Lena had only one choice—to get a job as a live-in domestic and begin saving for a return ticket. Two years passed and she was still far from her goal, but a lot can happen in two years—including a miracle. She met a young German immigrant at a church gathering and fell in love with him. When he asked her to marry him, she was deliriously happy, not because she had been rescued, but because she had been given the rare and wondrous gift of a second chance at love. Their marriage ultimately spanned forty years, producing five grandchildren and thirteen great-grandchildren.

"The first time I heard that story I was maybe five," Anne recalls. "I remembering looking at my grandmother as though she'd suddenly turned into a strange, exotic creature. I couldn't believe she could possibly have had a life with anybody but my grandpa. Later I thought it was so romantic that I actually wished something like it would happen to me. But then one day it suddenly struck me that if she'd married Thomas I wouldn't even *be* me. To a fifteen-year-old girl who thought she was invincible, that was quite a revelation!"

As time passed, Anne found herself returning to the story again and again, each time wondering what else it had to say to her. Did it explain whether events happen randomly or for a reason? Did it offer clues as to how to find joy in the wake of tragedy? Did it say something significant about hope, courage or love? It was not until the old story was retold at her grandmother's eightieth birthday party that the full magnitude of what it meant to be young, destitute and an ocean away from everything dear and familiar hit her full force.

"My grandmother became my hero that day," she says, her voice catching. "There she was, so tiny and frail, dressed in her best dress, looking so happy, surrounded by all of us who loved her so much. It was like I was seeing her for the first time. I was as stunned as if someone had just tossed a bucket of cold water in my face. I thought I'd never met anyone so brave in my entire life."

The story does not end there. Two years later Anne had occasion to revisit it yet again when her husband abruptly walked out, leaving her and their two children three hundred miles away from extended family. "Both of my kids were still in school, I hadn't worked in a decade, my degree was practically obsolete, and my ex was busily hiding his assets," Anne says. "It felt like the end of the world. By that time Grandma Lena had died, but it was as though I could hear her speaking to me through the story of Thomas. She told me, 'Yes, it's bad. It's terrible, but you can make it. I made it. Be strong, be strong, and you'll survive.' And that's exactly what happened."

We can spout platitudes by the score and tell our children anything we want them to believe. But long after the lectures are over, the stories will linger on. As we live out the stories of our own lives, we are guided by everything we have ever seen, heard, sensed or experienced. Though much of this rich mix lies hidden from view, it is always there just below the surface of consciousness, shaping our perception of the world, telling us what is good, what is taboo, what we can expect from other people and what the world and life are truly all about. A story overheard, a fleeting image, may lodge itself deeply in the mind, while a carefully planned story may blow away on the next day's breeze. Or the other way around. Since there is no way of knowing for sure, we have to be careful about what goes into the mix.

As our families' story keepers, we are much like the three workers described at the opening story of this chapter—the outcome depends a lot on our perception. We can choose to disbelieve the power of stories to create authentic, loving human beings. Or we can choose to make it our job to tack on neat, tidy little morals and use our stories as launch pads for lectures. Or we can elect instead to build, block by block, a thing of soaring beauty. Let's build a million cathedrals.

Things to Talk About

1. Explore the idea of stories' speaking louder than lectures. Can you think of a time when you effectively told a story to teach moral values? Can you think of a time when you missed the opportunity? How about a time when you tried, but wound up moralizing instead? What happened in these instances?

2. What does the word *hero* mean to you? Who are *your* heroes? Who are your family heroes? Why are all these people heroes?

Things to Do Right Now

1. Talk with your kids about heroes. Ask them what a hero is and who their heroes are.

2. Tell a family story where someone in the family becomes a hero. Ask your kids to think of other examples and tell their own hero stories.

3. The next chance you get, use a story to make a point about values. Be sure to have fun with it!

Four

Bandaging
the Soul
Stories & Healing

T HERE WAS ONCE A STORY I TOLD SO OFTEN IT BECAME KNOWN AS "THE story." "Have you told so-and-so 'the story' yet?" my husband would ask anytime I met someone new. We both knew it was a ridiculous question—it was almost impossible for me to know someone for more than forty-eight hours without telling "the story"—but it was a kind of ritual we observed. I think I must have told it at least fifty times over the course of fifteen years.

But then something happened that brought "the story" to a startling denouement. For a short while afterward, this new event served only to escalate my fixation, but eventually I stopped telling any of it. In fact, I can name three friends with whom I spend an inordinate amount of time who have not heard so much as a reference to either "the story" or its sequel. What happened? Easy—I did not need to tell it anymore.

When the soul cries out in pain or experiences a trauma that leaves it numb with shock, one of the ways it seeks to heal itself is through story. Psychologists have long known that the ability to articulate experience is critical to psychological well-being. This need to give voice, character, texture and meaning to the events that batter our psyches and rend our hearts is what sends us scrambling to the analyst's couch, the minister's study or the backyard fence. We long for a listening ear, someone who will help us begin the painful process of cleaning and bandaging our wounds.

"Groups like Alcoholics Anonymous are really storytelling groups," says professional storyteller Don Davis. "Members tell their story because it has a grip on them; they continue telling it until *they* get a grip on *it.*" And so it was for me and "the story." Somehow I had to come to terms with the cataclysmic event that forever branded the day after Thanksgiving, 1969, on my memory. I was just eighteen, a college freshman beginning a new job as a clerk at an upscale downtown department store. I landed a plum assignment in the high-visibility junior clothing department located just to the left of the store's main entrance, and I also got to work with Kathy, the college-age friend I had made during our week-long training program. As I think of that day now, it seems like one of those glass domes you shake to send a blizzard of iridescent snow swirling. As the flakes softly settle, a perfect, orderly world in microcosm reveals itself.

Inside the dome, Christmas trees gleaming with gold glass balls tower above a rack of mint-green sweaters. Packages wrapped in shiny gold paper lie heaped on a glass-topped table. Kathy and I, in violet dresses, glide around on high heels, waiting on customers and speaking in soft, modulated voices above the piped-in Christmas carols. We do so well that two hours into the morning our manager takes her coffee break and leaves us in charge. Now the dome cracks, and all the carefully ordered elegance sweeps out.

It happened very quickly, and I remember it exactly that way—a rapid-fire succession of stark images. A large elderly woman in a white dress staggered over to the table and heaved herself into a chair. I asked if I could help her, and she began to cough violently. Kathy sensed trouble and hurried over. The woman let out a long, low moan that rose to a wail. Tiny droplets of blood flew out of her mouth and spattered her dress. I fled to call an ambulance and returned to find—*freeze-frame*—Kathy kneeling on the floor in a puddle of red, cradling the woman's dead body in her arms.

It was not the first time I had witnessed sudden death. When I was ten, my best friend, Izzy, and I were walking home from the dime store when a teenage boy flipped off his speeding motorcycle, whizzed through the air and landed in a tangled heap at our feet. That time we talked about it. This time we didn't. Within an hour an ambulance took the woman to the morgue, the cleaning crew scrubbed away the blood, Kathy changed into a brand-new dress, and we were back at our registers, asking, "Will that be cash or charge?" The next day I was transferred across the aisle to jewelry, and Kathy was sent to the Summit Mall store. We never saw each other again.

At odd moments for the next fifteen years, the freeze-frame image of Kathy holding the dead woman's body would flash into my head—in the grocery store, in the shower, at the movies. I would tell and retell "the story," to come to terms less with the horror than with the sense of unreality. It was as though it had never happened. There were also two questions I asked myself again and again, *Why me?* and *Why again?*

In fall 1984 my husband and I hosted an open meeting at our home for families interested in international adoption. Five couples milled around our family room talking about infertility and the long waiting lists for American adoptions. I was especially drawn to one of them. We chatted for a while, and I asked the wife what she did for a living. She told me that she sold cosmetics for the department store chain where I had worked in college. I asked which store she worked at, and she told me the one at Summit Mall. "Have you worked there long?" I asked, my heart beginning to pound crazily.

"Since I was eighteen."

"Did you ever work at the downtown store?"

"Yeah, but only for a day."

"Was it the day after Thanksgiving 1969?"

She screamed in recognition.

I do not believe that meeting Kathy again was an accident. From the moment we looked at each other with the recognition of soldiers who once fought in the same trenches, I knew it was God's gift to us both, purposefully and lovingly bestowed at the perfect time. All those years I had told and retold "the story" were the beginning of the healing process. Telling it to Kathy and hearing her tell it to me was resolution for us both.

Because my experience in the department store occurred months before I met my husband and seven years before I had children, it is technically a personal story. Yet it became a family story for the simple reason that my family took ownership of it. When one family member has a story in need of healing, it is not uncommon for it to move from the realm of the personal to the realm of the familial, because at least indirectly the story affects the entire family. Each of us is the sum total of everything we have ever experienced. Our experiences impact how we relate to those we love and offer clues to who we are and why we behave as we do. Grandpa's brush with death during World War II, for example, can shed light on why he always celebrated life with such gusto, while Aunt Sadie's miserable passage from the old country might explain her refusal to take her children back to see their roots.

When the clan claims ownership of one member's story, members gather in solidarity and feel the power of group strength. If the tale is an unusual one, it is also a way to claim a bit of specialness by association. But most of all, it is a way for families to heal the one who is wounded. Through endless, patient listening to the story of Aunt Elizabeth's gall-bladder surgery, her family grants her the time, space and safety she needs to come to grips with an event that assaulted her body, mind and spirit. Though it may not be anyone's favorite tale, tolerance, generosity and love can transform a boring, mundane "operation story" into a thing of holiness.

There are times, of course, when the big stories belong to the entire family from the outset. A fire, a long layoff, a devastating illness or the death of a loved one sends *everybody* reeling with shock, grief and loss. Because we are a storytelling people, it is natural, healthy and necessary for us to gather together in times of trouble, stoke up the tribal fire and try to make sense of our battle scars. As you tell your story over and over, you give shape to the experience, take control of it, strengthen your connection with those who have shared it with you, and sift through the ashes of heartache to find the face of God.

Someone once asked Elie Wiesel, winner of the 1986 Nobel Peace Prize, why Jews feel so compelled to keep telling the story of the Holocaust. Wiesel responded, "We refuse to say yes to the executioner."[1] This refusal to allow the past to repeat itself, to allow the torment of a shattered soul to go unheard, is the first step toward healing. Story is the second. Story leads you back to the beginning. It takes you straight to the heart of both the experience and your emotions, where truth and meaning lie waiting to be discovered. Sometimes story even helps you find the kind of healing humor that baffles those who do not understand that God is present in our laughter as well as in our tears.

Healing Humor

Clare, a nurse who works the day shift in a nursing home, says that when she first went to work there five years ago as an idealistic new college graduate, the stories floating around the nursing station appalled her. Every morning the other nurses and aides would regale her with the latest installment in the continuing saga of Madalyn, an eighty-three-year-old woman suffering from Alzheimer's disease.

"One of the characteristics of Alzheimer's is something called sundown syndrome," Clare explains. "In many of these patients it manifests as extreme confusion, agitation and combativeness at the end of the day, just toward evening. Madalyn had it so bad that it often took two or three people to keep her from leaving the building. She had been a teacher years ago and was determined to get back to her job in West Virginia. She would always start out the same way—by coming out to the nurse's station wearing three sweaters and a slip, clutching her big black purse and demanding to buy a bus ticket to Wheeling."

Amid gales of laughter, the staff would recount how Madalyn had put her wig on backwards, tried to fend them off with her wooden cane and finally, in a frenzy of frustration, threatened to send them all to the principal's office if they did not "simmer down." At the time Clare did not crack a smile, yet today she is swapping stories with the best of them. What changed?

"I realized that I work with God's angels," she says simply. "These people see more tragedy in a day than most people see in a lifetime. They care so much that if they did not laugh they would drown in their own tears. Laughter is survival."

By telling your family "war stories," you learn the same lesson Clare learned at the nursing home. Instead of caving in under the weight of grief and despair, you laugh and regroup a little. Then you pick up your cross and move on.

Coming from an Irish background as I do, I have attended almost as many wakes and funerals as parties (sometimes only an insider can tell the difference between them). To see groups of people laughing uproariously one minute and sobbing piteously the next is as commonplace to me as the changing of the seasons. But I am deeply blessed to come from a people who understand that we never really say good-bye to those we continue to meet in our stories. Sheilagh, a young Irishwoman, told me that in the last six months she had attended two funerals: one for her uncle and another for her husband's uncle. The two events, she says, might as well have been held in different galaxies. At her Uncle Sean's wake, friends and family howled with merriment at the stories of how he once danced the jig on the hood of a car and just last summer on a trip back home to Ireland had reigned as the comic king of the nightly medieval dinner held at Bunratty Castle in County Limerick. "Oh, we laughed till we cried with the goings-on," she recalls, smiling at the memory. "But at my husband's uncle's funeral there was not a story to be heard. I walked across the cemetery on a beautiful summer day feeling as cold and barren as a Connemara moor. It was as though the poor man had vanished forever into that hole in the earth."

Those who have never felt the healing solace of humor often squirm with discomfort at the very mention of the departed's name. The thought of telling a story about that person is unthinkable. My friend Kathryn lost her thirteen-year-old son, Mac, when he rode his bike out of the family driveway straight into the path of a speeding car. In a misguided effort to protect his family from further grief, people avoided telling stories about him and even went to elaborate measures to avoid mentioning him at all. It was almost as if they were trying to pretend that he had never existed. But Kathryn knew that it was the laughter, the remembrance of good times, that would see her through the darkest night of the soul that any parent can endure. So she told the stories herself. Seven years later she is still telling them, and because of her, other grieving parents have learned to tell their own stories. One of the most poignant tells how her son's wacky sense of humor helped her find the right words to let him go.

Like most adolescent boys, Mac loved jokes, the sillier the better. He loved to ask his mom, "Does your face hurt?" When she would say no, he would flash her a grin as wide as the world and say, "Well, it's sure killin' me!" Just before the casket was closed on the day of his funeral, Kathryn looked down at her only son and whispered, "Does your face hurt, Mac?" To the deafening silence, she responded, "Well, it's sure killing me."

Healing stories told during times of grief, and laughter rendered bittersweet by pain—both are gifts of a gracious God, a God who weeps right along with you in your sorrow. Each time you tell your stories and laugh through your tears, you let go of a few more jagged shards of grief. Those who listen and identify with your loss help you sweep them up and in the process relinquish some of their own pain as well. Telling the stories also allows you to return, if only momentarily, to ordinary time—to the time before your heart was broken. Kathryn laughs with infectious delight as she tells the story of how every morning before he raced out the door to catch the school bus, Mac would bang out on the piano (*bang* being the operative word) the tune to "The Entertainer," the theme song of the old Robert Redford film *The Sting,* and describes Mac's pet alligator named Carl, who lived in the bathtub. Her stories are a grace period (in both senses of the term), a temporary time-out to celebrate life in the midst of death.

Healing humor can also pour its gentle balm on life's smaller aches, the times when you have been bruised by conditions you feel powerless to change. Since both of my girls are Korean, they have experienced the hurt of being singled out. It is less a matter of overt ridicule and more of thoughtlessness, subtle racism and well-meaning kindness that misses the mark by a mile and a half. Some of our most hilarious moments come from reliving these scenes. There is the time Moira was working at an outdoor event, ladling chili, and a man sauntered over and asked, "What's on the menu today, chop suey?"

The time she was working at our family store and a customer picked up a pair of Chinese scissors and asked, "Your relatives make these things?"

The time when she was a baby and a high-school principal asked me whether I thought she would find it difficult to learn to speak English.

The countless times a stranger has looked at her picture and exclaimed, "What a pretty little China doll!" (She is twenty-one.)

The time when I was shopping with her at an upscale department store and a woman came over and asked me if I was married to a doctor. Puzzled, I replied that I was not, but that I was curious as to why she asked. "Oh, because of your daughter," she said brightly. "The hospitals are full of Asian doctors these days."

And the time last winter when a woman we did not know approached Caitie at Wal-Mart, threw her arms around her and told her how "wonderful" her parents must be to have adopted her and how glad she was it had happened. We tell these stories and laugh, not so much to poke fun at ignorance as to share the sting of racism and embarrassing sentimentality. The stories are collective Band-Aids because when one of us gets scraped, the rest of us cry ouch too.

Healing Relationships

Telling your stories can heal much more than a battered heart or wounded feelings. It can also heal your relationships. One after another, people have shared examples of times when stories gave them insight into family members they had previously been unable to welcome into their hearts. Mary Lynn told of a great-aunt she had always viewed as stern and unyielding. This aunt had virtually raised her mother, a fact that had always made Mary Lynn sad because she saw her mother's upbringing as cold and unloving. It was not until she had children of her own that she finally began to listen to the old stories and understand how dearly her mother had loved her caretaker.

Another woman, Angela, said that she had always enjoyed a close relationship with her great-aunt Sophia. But the day she joyfully announced her intention to adopt a baby from Guatemala, Aunt

Sophia became as upset as if Angela had decided to defect to a communist country. At first she tried to talk her out of proceeding with the home study by pointing out the risks of any adoption. When that proved futile, she escalated her efforts by zeroing in on racial and cultural differences. By the time she was finished, her relationship with her niece was strained to the breaking point.

Angela's father's kept it from snapping. Privately, he told Angela stories of the prejudice that Aunt Sophia had experienced as a young woman. Because she was Italian, people called her "dago" and "wop" and sometimes shunned her. Refusing to accept a Latino child into the family was her way of dealing with memories that had not lost their sting fifty years later.

"All that happened back in the 1940s," Angela says, "but I was still surprised to hear it. In a way it seemed strange to me that somebody who had experienced such bigotry would turn around and inflict it on somebody else, but in another way I could understand it too. I guess it was some sort of retaliation. At any rate, my dad's stories helped me separate this one issue from the whole of our relationship. My aunt died last year, and it still hurts me that she never came to know and love my daughter, but it doesn't negate all the years of love she gave me. She honestly thought she was acting in my best interests."

Of course, not everyone succeeds in putting aside differences as successfully as Angela did, but stories can still soften the harshness even when reconciliation, at least for the moment, seems impossible. Last year, Caroline's father died and left a considerable estate that she should have shared equally with her older brother, Dave. But due to complex wheeling and dealing on Dave's part, however, she wound up getting cheated out of a large percentage of what was rightfully hers. As painful as the loss of potential funding for her children's college education was, it paled in comparison to the devastating sense of betrayal she felt at having been conned by her own brother.

"After I found out what he had done, I felt like the world had split in two and I'd fallen into the crack, " she says. "I felt like you couldn't trust anything or anybody. For a while I actually hated him. At this point—it's been three years—I'm past that, but I still don't see how we can ever have a relationship again. The only thing that gives me any hope is a story I tell about something that happened at the funeral. In that one story at least, you've just gotta love the guy."

When Dave became a teenager and started dating, her father would invariably slip some money into his shirt pocket, chuckle and say, "A few bucks for the road, Davie." At the funeral home when the family filed in for the final viewing, Dave stunned everyone when he pulled out his wallet and took out a five-dollar bill. With twelve pairs of eyes watching, he carefully folded it, tucked it into his father's shirt pocket and said, "A few bucks for the road, Dad."

In a sense, each of these stories is a cautionary tale, a warning not to allow hardening of the heart in difficult relationships. When told in a nonthreatening way, in a spirit of love for the listener, they hold tremendous power. And very often it is the teller of the tale who is healed.

Cautionary Tales

There is a wonderful old Armenian saying that goes, "Three apples fell from heaven: one for the teller, one for the listener and one for the one who heeds the tale." It refers, of course, to cautionary tales, the stories you tell straight from the core of your greatest sorrow, fear or love, in hopes of keeping your loved ones safe. In telling these stories, you try to pass on the insights born of your own experience and warn the listener to avoid making the same mistakes you or someone you care about made in the past. Healing comes not only through the telling of the story itself but also through the transformation of pain and regret into wisdom and love.

Not long after the release of his remarkable film *Schindler's List,* producer/director Steven Spielberg began a project called Survivors of the Shoah (*shoah* is the Hebrew word for Holocaust), which elevated the cautionary tale to a tribute to human dignity. Seventy-five staff members, plus forty-five trained interviewers, videographers and other volunteers, are at this writing traveling to sixteen regions of the world to record on camera the stories of death-camp survivors. When they finish compiling the massive number of interviews, probably in 1997, the Survivors of the Shoah Visual History Foundation will have captured more than one hundred thousand hours of individual survivor testimony that will be given to repositories in New York, Los Angeles and Jerusalem, as well as to Yale University in New Haven, Connecticut, and the Holocaust Museum in Washington, D.C. "The majority of Holocaust survivors are in their seventies and eighties," Spielberg says. "The window for capturing their testimonies is closing fast. It is essential that we see their faces, hear their voices and understand that the horrendous events of the Holocaust happened to people and were committed by people."[2]

Spielberg is right. Facts and figures do not tell us what we need to know. Old black-and-white news footage comes closer, but too often it makes us shudder and turn away. It is the eyes, the voices, the *stories* of those who have lived through the horror that in the end will compel us to listen. They are abominable stories, gruesome, beyond our comprehension, but sacred too because they offer humanity the chance for healing and redemption. Every Holocaust story is a family story in the most cosmic sense because in telling how history ravaged one family, it tells how it ravaged us all.

Though few cautionary tales are as enormous as the Holocaust, every family tells them, whether they realize it or not. Most are simple stories about love, relationships, health, raising children and surviving in the world. A father warns his son to keep his grades up and go to college by sharing his battle stories of surviving in a world where getting a job right after high school and working your way up through the ranks of the same company until retirement has gone the way of the horse and buggy. A mother tells the story of being stood up for the prom to keep her daughter from putting too much faith in a relationship with a boy who clearly cannot be trusted. According to psychologist Barbara H. Fiese of Syracuse University, mothers tend to tell stories of affiliation by recalling experiences that involve caring and belonging, while the stories fathers tell center primarily on achievements. But whoever is telling them, cautionary tales told with gentleness and caring are acts of love because when you tell them, you willingly return to difficult or painful experiences and emotions to heal and shelter the people you value.[3]

Tough Stories

Sometimes, though, it is too difficult to return. Perhaps not enough time has passed or you still have not come to grips with what happened to be able to share it without allowing raw emotions to confuse the point. Perhaps you question whether any good can come from sifting through old ashes. How can you determine whether it is an act of healing grace to tell a tough story or whether it is better to keep silent? This is the question that haunts Greg, the father we met in chapter three who struggled with feelings of childhood deprivation when his children complained about their trip to Florida.

Growing up in Greg's childhood home was like growing up in a war zone. He spent most of it creeping around in camouflage fatigues, hoping to remain invisible. There was no telling when his silent, distant father would explode in fury or when his mercurial mother would let fly yet another torrent of physical and emotional abuse. His parents' house was a house of secrets and rage, a place where he never felt safe. When he moved out of it at age eighteen, he swore he would never go back, but in order to give his sons grandparents, he did.

"My parents are holiday grandparents," he says flatly. "They don't know my kids any better than they knew me. But they trot out the token gifts and make the right noises a couple times a year, so at least you have to give them that. The kids know it's a sham, but in a way they care about them. How can I tell my children what it was really like for me, aside from the poverty stuff? Sometimes I think they'd never believe it. My parents have metamorphosed into two little old people who wouldn't hurt a fly. There's a part of me that says let it go, but another part of me wants my children to know that I struggle being their dad because I had no role models. What should I do? I don't know. I really don't know."

To find answers to thorny questions such as these, I turned to Elaine Wynne, a professional storyteller and psychotherapist in private practice in Minneapolis. For the past twenty years she has told stories as an entertainer, and for the past fifteen she has combined storytelling with therapy. She began her career at Minneapolis Children's Medical Center working with children suffering from chronic and acute illnesses, an ideal environment to begin pursuing storytelling as a path to healing. The first thing she told me is that there *are* no easy, textbook answers when it comes to disclosure.

Every case is different and unique, Wynne says, and parents in doubt might want to talk it over with a counselor or a clergyman before telling *any* tough stories to their kids, because there are many things children simply should not have to deal with. But she makes an exception when the child could be in danger of being harmed. Telling a cautionary tale, even if it is a tough one, to protect a child from any sort of abuse is not only acceptable, it is essential. Yet even then she cautions parents to link the story with other less difficult stories that also have a protection theme and not to let it stand starkly on its own. When protection issues are not a factor, she still stresses the importance of proceeding carefully, especially in situations where the parent has not reached a place where he or she can tell a tough story in a spirit of acceptance and/or forgiveness. Ask yourself why you feel it necessary to tell the story. Is it for *you* or for the child? Who stands to be hurt? Is the child old enough to understand? Can this story bring about either affirmation or redemption?

"I don't think we should reinvent the past to make people look good," Wynne says. "But if you're still in a rage over some aspect of the past, then I think it's better to tread lightly. If a child asks a difficult question, it's better to be honest and say, 'I'm having a hard time telling happy stories about that right now.'"

In her practice Wynne often tells her clients stories to help them catch hold of a new idea or insight. She also listens to their stories and, if they desire, helps them find a way to restructure the painful ones. One of the most important things to remember about tough stories, she notes, is that we revisit them at different points in our lives, each time bringing a wealth of new experiences and emotions that color our perceptions and shed new light on the dark places. For example, at one point in our lives we may say, "My father was a cruel, unloving man." Later we might say, "My father was cold and harsh, but he provided for us well and we could depend on him." Still later, "My father wasn't the most affectionate or fun-loving man, but I know that in his way he loved us." And finally, "My father did the best he could." Healing a painful past is a gradual process that can sometimes last a lifetime. Often it is necessary to work out the painful stories with a professional before introducing them to your family.

I talked with one woman who successfully restructured her story of a lonely, abusive childhood. She asked me not to mention even her first name because she has chosen not to share the full scope of the abuse with her children. Like Greg's children, they maintain a relationship with their grandparents that she does not want jeopardized. When they ask for stories about "Grandma and Grandpa and when you were little," she tells them about small, neutral events or focuses on moments of fleeting happiness. "I don't feel it's lying to them. Almost every family has *some* good times. At least I'd think so, as few people are ever totally bad," she says. "My children do know that my childhood was no walk in the park—I mean, they've seen their grandparents behave dysfunctionally on a smaller scale—but I can see no reason for them to know the whole thing. As time has passed and I have worked through the painful stories, I've actually found one about my father that's rather touching in its way."

For as long as she could remember, she wanted to be a newspaper reporter. When she graduated from high school, she badly wanted to go away to a top-notch journalism school, but her mother was adamant that she stay home and go to a community college. For weeks tensions escalated, until finally they erupted in a scene she would rather not remember. The next afternoon when her father came home from work, he tossed an envelope in her lap. "What's this?" she asked.

"Your application for the journalism school," he said gruffly. "You better get busy and get it done."

"But what about Mom?"

"Never mind," he replied, "I took care of it." She went to journalism school.

Somehow over the years the story got lost, buried under a mountain of painful memories, harsh words and recriminations. It was not until she told her difficult stories to her husband, her therapist and her parish priest that she made what she calls an astounding discovery. "I realized that my parents weren't born the way they are. Someone had to have done something to *them*. It was like a light bulb went on in my head. It opened the door to seeing them in a more accepting light. Once I could do that, I remembered the college story. I don't know whether I've truly forgiven my parents yet, but I want to, and this story is a step in the right direction. How can I not feel some warmth for the man who gave me my heart's desire?"

In his audiotape *The Power of Stories*, philosopher Sam Keen points out four ways to tell a story: as a tragedy that is designed to inspire pity; as a romance that focuses on triumph over pain and elicits admiration from the audience; as irony that is told with cynicism rather than as tragedy or triumph; or as a comedy, which, of course, inspires laughter. The whole world, Keen says, can change with the modality you use to tell your story.[4]

Margaret, a professional storyteller from Pennsylvania, learned this firsthand when she told at a family party the story of Uncle Casey, who was in some ways the family "black sheep." Uncle Casey made his living by traveling around the country showing movies on the sides of barns in agricultural communities too small and too remote to support a regular indoor theater. Though his knowledge of movies and movie stars was prodigious, what he knew and loved best was swimming. Whenever he tooled around the back roads of the Midwest, he always kept his eye out for an inviting swimming hole. The second he spotted one, he immediately pulled off to the side of the road and dove in, no matter where he was supposed to be. The problem is, between all this swimming and movie showing, Uncle Casey often was not as available to his family as they wished him to be, and there were a lot of hurt, angry feelings. Margaret chose to tell his story as a comedy. It brought down the house and also brought about visible signs of healing as his family began to see him in the light of a well-meaning, somewhat eccentric "character."

Parents like Greg, who lack a blueprint for parenting and have not yet found a way to recast their own tragedies, can find it helpful to share stories with other parents, Wynne says. Through the process of telling stories from the perspective of both your child self and your parent self and through listening to other parents tell how they were raised and how they are raising their own children, you gain perspective, learn to celebrate your triumphs and begin to move past your failures. It also helps you draw up your own blueprint for parenthood. Linda, a mother of three grown children who volunteers her time through her church to mentor parents who struggle to break the cycle of abuse in their families, shared her experiences. When she began, she says, she was astonished by the effect some of her stories had on her listeners. One story in particular, which she used to feel was almost too commonplace to be significant, never fails to elicit a strong response from her audience.

One day, some twenty years ago, Linda was in her bedroom getting ready to go to the grocery store when her three young children, all under the age of ten, caught a toad that they slowly ripped apart in an effort to see what toads are made of. They poked and prodded until suddenly the youngest child realized the enormity of what they had done—the toad did not hop off into the bushes when they finished their experiment. Hysterical, she ran to get her mother.

What amazes young parents is how Linda dealt with the two older culprits. Rather than succumb to her desire to turn into a wild woman, she decided to turn the incident into a lesson they would never forget. To this day all three kids tell the story of how they had to miss their weekly treat of having a donut at the grocery store to stay home with their father and learn about toads. By the time they were finished, she says, they knew more about the warty amphibians than they ever wanted to!

Stories and Transition

Cautionary tales and other healing stories can be told anytime, but times of transition bring them to the fore. Births, graduations, moving days, weddings, new jobs, retirement and funerals cause us to pause along life's path and look back over our shoulder at where we have been. Whether you acknowledge it or not, some deep part of your being knows that even the joyful transitions serve as reminders of both the passage of time and your own mortality. At your daughter's wedding you laugh and tell stories of her childhood. You reminisce about other family weddings and perhaps tell a cautionary tale gleaned from your own experience of marriage. The day is warm and fun and filled with a sense of community, but once the music stops and the last guest has left, you find that within the joy lies buried a kernel of deep sadness. You cry, you mourn for the child that once was. Then you take a deep breath and (perhaps in a second, maybe the next morning) probe the kernel of sadness and discover a seed of joy hidden inside. In ushering out one season of life, you welcome in the richness of the next.

Transition times often call for stories that uplift, the kinds of tales that say, "Yes, yes, everything is going to be fine. I did it. Cousin Mike did it. You can do it too." When a door seems to slam shut, stories open a window, let in a breath of fresh air, and show you what wonders wait as soon as you get up the courage to go back out into the world. They are the stories you tell when your son is afraid to start his new school and your sister loses her job.

What is interesting about all stories is that their very structure mimics life's transitional nature. Resolution inevitably follows conflict, just as the end always follows the beginning. But as a veteran of both life and stories, you know that no sooner are the words *the end* spoken than something else happens and a new story begins. And so it goes until you reach the biggest transition of all—the passage from this earthly life to life eternal.

Pat Stropko-O'Leary, director of the hospice program in Medina, Ohio, observes that death forces us all to revisit the stories of our lives. Whether we are rich or poor, mighty or humble, we all seek meaning for our existence at the end, and we find it in our stories. Not long ago, Pat asked me whether the tough times or the happy ones have exerted greater influence on my life. Immediately I replied, "The tough ones." But later I realized something. The tough times gave me strength and compassion, but I found hope and awe in the good ones. To make us whole, we need both our tragedies and our comedies, as well as everything in between. Philosopher and theologian Thomas Aquinas (1225-1274) once said that it is delight that changes people most. Can it be that the tough stories cannot transform and heal us until we allow them to give us joy?

Years ago, when Pat worked as a nurse for a hospice program in a different city, she took care of a dying man whose great tragedy was his estrangement from the son who shamed the family by landing in the state penitentiary. For weeks the hospice staff urged him to go to the prison and visit his son, but the man adamantly refused. Finally, when it seemed that death was imminent, he had a change of heart. But by then he could no longer travel. Desperate to help him find closure, the hospice staff pleaded with prison officials to allow the son to come home. The answer was no. Prisoners were not allowed to visit private homes, including their own or their family's.

But the hospice workers refused to be deterred. They arranged instead to have the father transported by ambulance to their facility and the son brought there also, under armed guard. On the day of the meeting, the prison vehicle pulled up at the hospice door at the precise hour, and the conditions of the visit were spelled out. Two guards would remain present throughout the meeting, and it would terminate in exactly one hour. To offer the dying man support and to monitor his oxygen and other medical equipment, Pat and the hospice social worker would remain present also.

Imagine this scene! Imagine seeing your father for the first time in years, shrunken by disease and laboring for every breath. Imagine seeing your son shackled and dressed in the bright orange jumpsuit of the prison system, knowing it is for the last time. Imagine revisiting decades of painful stories as four strangers look on and the clock ticks thunderously in your ears. It is unfathomable that holiness could ever find its way into such a setting, but holiness is not easily deterred either. Before the hour was over, Pat and the social worker had to leave the room—it seemed an abomination to bear witness to such sacred, wrenching joy. Not long after the son returned to prison, his father died.

Alida Gersie, an author who has written voluminously about storytelling, offers the image of the "story bag." Each person, she maintains, has an imaginary bag that contains the memories, experiences and stories of a lifetime. Into it you slip the day you were married. Into it goes the night the basement flooded. In goes the day you stood at the kitchen window and marveled at the red head of a woodpecker. At the end of your life it is time to untie the string, scatter the contents across the bed and see what you have collected. And there it is—treasure: not only in the moments of tragedy and transcendence but also in the brown bag lunches you packed for the kids and the red geraniums you planted in the yard.[5] "Everyday events, put into perspective, reveal the meaning of our lives," Pat says. "And the ordinary becomes extraordinary."

In a very real sense, your story bag is a medicine bag filled with strong remedies for easing the pain of the heart, healing the wounds of the spirit and preventing you from leaving this life with no understanding of why you were here. The next time you feel sad, lonely or dispirited, try this prescription: Take two stories and call someone you love. You don't even have to wait until morning.

Things to Talk About

1. Think about the tough stories you find yourself repeating again and again. Why do you think you tell them? What would it take to heal them?

2. How does your family handle bad times? Is the concept of "healing humor" part of your tradition? Would you like it to be?

3. Reflect on the idea of cautionary tales. What cautionary tales have been told to you? Which ones do you tell? What is the response of your audience? How might you tell them in a less threatening way?

Things to Do Right Now

1. Make a family story bag. Use your imagination and allow each family member to contribute something to its design. Use whatever materials and mediums you desire to make a bag that best reflects your family's unique identity. When you are finished, attach a string or a ribbon to one corner and hang it in a prominent place. Anybody who has a story to remember writes a few words about it on a piece of paper and puts it in the bag. Plan a special day to empty the bag, tell the stories, and talk about what they mean to you. Make it a special event.

2. Rewrite a tough story from your life. Start with something small and see if you can retell it in such a way that it is more comedy than tragedy. If that is not possible, try telling it from the point of view of the other person. Share any insights.

Five

Finding God at the Fireside
Stories & Spirituality

T HE DOCTOR DID NOT MINCE WORDS—NO MORE MANUAL LABOR FOR HA Thuc. My husband and I looked at each other in dismay, registering exactly the same thought. The house of cards that we had built so carefully for our family of Vietnamese refugees since their arrival six months earlier was about to come crashing down around our ears. No job for Ha Thuc meant no rent money. And no rent money for a house of their own meant that he and all seven of his family members would soon be returning to *our* house. The thought of ten people plus our brand-new baby (who was still operating on Korean time two weeks after her arrival) residing under the same roof for more than a few days was enough to send me hurtling toward hysteria.

Late that night we sat in the living room and weighed our possibilities. Ha Thuc spoke only fair English. He had neither a car nor the means to buy one, and the vast majority of jobs were in either Akron or Cleveland, both a good half-hour's drive away. In Saigon he had repaired office machinery for the National Cash Register Company, but in our small town of two thousand people a full-time business machine repairman was in less demand than a full-time clock winder. Worse yet, prejudice and strong feelings about the Vietnam War ran so rampant that landing him the factory job had been nothing short of miraculous. Possibilities? We clearly did not have any. "If his back gets any worse, we're going to have even bigger problems." Eric warned, echoing my own thoughts. "With no health or disability insurance, he could be in serious trouble. We've *got* to get him out of that factory."

The next morning I got on the phone and frantically called every business machine company in the phone book, telling myself that maybe if we nailed down the job, the transportation would work itself out somehow. But eight calls later, the answer was a resounding "no thanks." That left us with two choices—Ha Thuc could either go on welfare or hang onto his poorly paid manufacturing job. He elected to increase the painkillers and hang on.

Meanwhile we prayed, networked and scoured the classifieds, but a shaky six weeks went by and still nothing materialized. Then one Saturday afternoon a tired-looking man in a rumpled suit came into our family store and mentioned to my husband that he had heard we owned a private collection of early Ohio long rifles and asked to see it.

Eric hesitated. For security reasons he never took strangers upstairs to the mini-museum where the muzzleloaders shared space with his father's antique toy collection and a large case of Indian relics and artifacts. It was the busiest time of the day, customers were crowding the showroom, and the phone was shrilling off the hook. Yet there was something about the guy . . . "Sure, come on up," he heard himself say.

After viewing the collection and talking knowledgeably about American history, the man thanked Eric for being so gracious. "I really appreciate it," he said. "This is the first time I've relaxed in months. I'm so stressed out at work, you wouldn't believe it. I've been trying for weeks to a fill a position and it's the next thing to impossible. You wouldn't know any minorities skilled in business machine repair, would you?"

For a second Eric could only stare at him. "Would a Vietnamese do?" he asked when he recovered his voice.

"Sure, but what are my chances of finding *that* unlikely combination?"

Two days later Ha Thuc had the job. On his first day he proved so skillful that he moved up several pay levels to a position that provided medical benefits for his entire family. That evening a driver's education teacher at the high school volunteered to teach him how to drive, and a family with few resources of its own offered to sell him a good used car at a practically giveaway price. Donations turned up to pay part of the cost, and Eric and I made up the difference. Within two weeks he was a licensed driver behind the wheel of his own seven-year-old, low-mileage Buick, holding down a career-level position with a national company!

Viewing this sequence of events from a distance of twenty years, it seems like an exquisitely choreographed ballet: the conductor raises his baton, the orchestra begins to play, and each dancer leaps into a perfectly executed *grand jeté* on the downbeat. I do not know how many times we have told that story, but each time both Eric and I are amazed all over again by the incredible odds.

The story of Ha Thuc is a textbook example of sacred storytelling, the holy work of sharing with others the presence of God in our daily lives. Whenever you tell a sacred story, you attempt to express the inexpressible, a task that on the surface may seem about as foolish as trying to peel a rainbow off the sky. Surely if the poets struggle to find the perfect phrase or image to describe the creative mind of God and still come up empty, it is ridiculous to think that an accountant, a father, a hair stylist or a child could succeed at turning wonder into words. Yet we have no choice but to try. All that exists before story is the experience itself, so story is as close to your encounter with God's grace and glory as it is possible to get. Besides, the heart cannot possibly hold so much awe without succumbing to the natural urge to share it.

Each time you tell a sacred story you give your audience two things: a gift and an invitation. The gift is yourself, and the invitation is the listeners' chance to personalize your experience. Although it is tempting to pull your audience directly into your own emotions and point of view, the goal is to lead them into their own. The ideal response is "Oh yes, I see! It's like the time that I . . ." rather than "Wow, that's an incredible thing that happened to you!" By showing God at work in *your* life, you show God at work in theirs.

But sometimes when we try to convey our experience of the sacred, we make the mistake of thinking that sacred stories by definition require religious language. We layer on biblical passages, weave in homilies, and talk as though we are so transformed by our experience that we now stand in the hallowed position of being able to speak for God instead of in praise of God. Certainly there are times when the language of religion is required to adequately express a profound moment, but there are many, many other times when the simple language of the heart is enough. God's glory shines just as brightly through shrieks of hilarity and tears of compassion as through religiosity. Sacred stories explore such themes as friendship, forgiveness, love, joy, rebirth, reconciliation, conversion, creativity, creation and unabashed fun. Since each story, as well as each audience, requires its own special language, imagery and style, it becomes your challenge to find the one that best conveys your *genuine* experience of the sacred. The best way—the only way—to tell a sacred story is authentically, from the heart of who *you* are, while allowing others to do the same.

I love that old saying "God is in the details" because it so aptly sums up the philosophy of sacred stories. If God is there in the *thump, thump* of the basketball on the cement driveway, in the heady purple scent of lilacs wafting into the house from the bush by the back door, and in the tiny white pearl of a tooth emerging from the pink ridge of a baby's gum, then all you really need to convey God's grandeur is your own five senses. Richly detailed stories, told with neither affectation nor agenda, feed your family's spiritual life just as the meals you cook (or send out for!) fuel their physical ones.

In his book *Patterns of Grace: Human Experience as the Word of God,* Tom F. Driver, theology professor and student of renowned theologian Paul Tillich, writes, "I find myself not only agreeing that theology originates in stories (and should itself tell more of them), but also thinking that all knowledge comes from a mode of understanding that is *dramatic.*"[1]

Andrew Greeley, Roman Catholic priest and sociologist, takes it a step further. In his book *Religion as Poetry* he says, "Religion *is* story, story before it is anything else, story after it is anything else, story born from experience, coded in symbol, reinforced in the self, and shared with others to explain life and death."[2]

Clearly, one of the most effective ways to foster your family's spiritual growth is to light a fire under their imaginations, engage their emotions and leave them with an experience that works its way into the fabric of their beings. It is much the same principle as the one we explored in chapter three about using stories to teach children moral values. If you faithfully feed the rich internal mix of the psyche with stories, the natural process of fermentation will do the rest.

In an article about storytelling for the *Christian Ministry* magazine, professional storyteller Cindy Guthrie of Port Huron, Michigan, offers a delightful example of what transpires when something happens to evoke a story that has been thoroughly assimilated by the listener. A newscaster covering the scene of a devastating tornado reported that just as their house blew off its foundation, one member of a family of survivors spontaneously cried out, "Auntie Em! Auntie Em!" Any time you tell a sacred story to your family naturally and vividly, you set the stage for them to internalize it just as completely as that tornado survivor had absorbed *The Wizard Of Oz.*

Guthrie also makes a fascinating comparison between storytelling and Christianity. The two are ideally suited to one another, she maintains, because storytelling is an incarnate art and Christianity is an incarnate religion. Just as Jesus is the Word made flesh, you, the storyteller, use your physical body through your voice and gestures to give flesh and blood to your words. When the incarnation is complete, the story and its truth live on in the being of the listener.

I would venture to say that the storytelling process and Christianity share yet another commonality—mystery. Why a simple story holds vast, unlimited potential remains as mysterious as why the green tips of daffodils poke bravely through the snow. We do not really *know* why a small story sometimes changes the world while a big one is forgotten. Or why a story that has long slipped out of consciousness continues to influence our lives. Or why a story strikes a resonant chord in one person and wafts past another unheeded. But neither can we comprehend infinity. Or Trinity. Or the afterlife. All we know is that if we combine the two mysteries—if we use our stories to help answer life's most puzzling, fundamental and universal questions—we can part the veil, if only for a moment, between this world and the one to come.

Entering the Mystery

Growing up Catholic, I was surrounded by stories of mystery. My father talked of the scent of roses that suddenly and inexplicably filled the air the night his little sister Theresa died in their home on the island of Maui. Every time I heard him tell that story it thrilled me. It also made perfect sense because she had been named in honor of the French Carmelite nun Thérèse of Lisieux, the Little Flower of Jesus, who loved roses and died at the age of twenty-four. Because stories of wondrous occurrences had been doled out to me like peanut butter and jelly sandwiches ever since I was old enough to comprehend them, I never once asked, "Could that really have happened?" I simply accepted that it had and willingly allowed myself to be led deeper into the mystery of God.

I love these mystical kinds of family stories and gather them up like fallen chestnuts to be squirreled away for the wintry seasons of the heart. Yet it is crucial not to confuse mystery with mysticism. There is as much mystery in the first time your baby smiles at you with recognition as there is in the scent of unseen roses. There is mystery in the story of Ha Thuc, too, as well as in every other story in this book because each one shows God at work in the lives of human beings. The changing of the seasons, enlightenment, small unexplainable moments of sudden joy, love—all of these are deep, profound mysteries. But because we have become accustomed to them, we deem them "ordinary" and reserve our awe for the otherwordly, when in fact the otherwordly is as ordinary as chicken soup. Though we may not catch many glimpses of it on earth, it is nonetheless *there,* coexisting with the very mysteries we take for granted. Yet I heard enough stories of strange "coincidences" during my fifty interviews to believe that God understands our need to be stopped in our tracks sometimes, frozen with astonishment.

On Christmas Eve 1995, when other families in Dalton, Ohio, were joyously gathering to celebrate the birth of one mother's Child, Sue's family was huddling together in shock and anguish. That very evening they had received the staggering news that her sister Janice's twenty-four-year-old son, Todd, had been killed in an automobile accident. Just four months earlier he had begun a job teaching third grade. And now in a single, blinding moment a life that had gleamed with so much promise was over.

Soon after the funeral, family members began telling each other stories of vivid, comforting dreams in which Todd spoke to them. Everyone had experienced one, even the nieces and nephews— everyone, that is, except his mother, Janice. How could it be, she asked endlessly, that her son, with whom she had shared such closeness, would speak to everyone else and forget about her? As the stories continued to pile up, a growing sense of confusion compounded her grief.

One evening in late January she was sitting in her darkened living room, crying. Then out of the corner of her eye she noticed motion by the dim light at the window. Getting up to investigate, she pulled back the curtain and stared, transfixed, at a magnificent yellow-and-black butterfly, unlike any she had ever seen. All that protected its delicate, beating wings from the bitter wind and six inches of newly fallen snow were two sheets of thermopane glass. The next day she did some research and learned that it was most likely a swallowtail, a variety that is not as abundant in Ohio as the familiar orange-and-black monarch.

Two days later the huge yellow butterfly was still residing in the living room when a friend of Todd's who had survived the accident dropped by to bring her some of her son's belongings. Among them was a sheaf of papers that included some poetry. Janice scanned the first poem and let out a gasp. *Once I had a dream that I was a butterfly who thought he was a man. Or was I a man who thought he was a butterfly?* There was no question that Todd had written these words of the poet Lao-tzu. The handwriting was almost as familiar as her own.

As I tell that extraordinary little story, an unmistakable surge of hope flutters in my heart. Of course I realize that there is a perfectly plausible, if somewhat unusual, explanation for the butterfly's unseasonable appearance. Swallowtails winter in the chrysalis stage. A caterpillar must have gotten into the house, formed a chrysalis and, responding to the warmth of the furnace, hatched prematurely. But entomology is beside the point when it comes to sacred stories! It does not matter *how* the butterfly happened to be there at the perfect moment. All that matters is that it was.

Like the butterfly, sacred stories break free of their cocoon and take flight at the perfect moment. When the season is right and the heart of the listener is ready, truth will invariably transcend questions, doubt and even entomology. The essential truth of the butterfly story is simply that God so loves the world that he sees the sorrow of a mother's heart and sends her a measure of peace. That's all. And that's everything.

As you begin to find God at the fireside through your own family stories, it is important not to get so hung up on facts and probabilities that you miss the metaphor and thus the message. Not long after I heard the butterfly story, I passed the office of our local hospice and saw, as though for the first time, the blue butterfly on its sign. The butterfly has become an almost universal symbol of hope, a reminder that we leave this earthly life to fly again in beauty in another. God, it would seem, understands this and speaks to us through symbols we recognize.

A Matter of Truth

Whenever you begin to ponder the question of mystery, sooner or later the issue of truth surfaces. This is more of a problem for some of us than it is for others. Poets, artists and natural storytellers do not seem to care too much how butterflies hatch and what the probability is that a swallowtail would shed its cocoon in the dead of winter. But the scientists and pragmatists among us find it difficult to accept any story until it is clearly and logically proven to be possible. I am a natural storyteller, while my husband is a pragmatist. But that has not stopped us from telling each other stories. We agreed long ago to allow each other to approach story from our own individual perspectives.

That is all you *can* do when you are telling stories to your family. As the storyteller, you have the job of telling the story—*not* interpreting it for anyone else. Each listener will take from it what she needs, a process that can span a lifetime as she revisits the story at many different points along the way. This constant revisiting is precisely why it is so important to keep telling your stories over and over, even if they seem to be rolling off your kids like rainwater. You never know when the heart will suddenly open and allow an ignored, maligned or previously puzzling story to suddenly take root. It might be the second or ninth or twenty-third time you tell it.

As you become more and more attuned to the storytelling process, you will begin to notice the influence of imagination. Tom F. Driver contends that *all* stories are fictitious. "A true story is as fictive as the rest," he says, "for without imagination the story does not arise." Think about those infamous "fish stories" that avid sportsmen love to tell. It does not matter whether the focus of an individual story is fishing, hunting or playing racquetball—every time it is told the accomplishment grows a little grander until eventually it qualifies for the *Guinness Book of World Records*. Natural storytellers embellish constantly, often without even being aware of it. As they leap into the story, their eyes sparkle, their voices rise several octaves, and their gestures become more and more dramatic as their imaginations kick into high gear. I know, because I do it all the time.

"That's not what happened, Mom!" Caitie, our resident stickler for accuracy, will cry. Each time she says this, I stop in midembellishment and stare at her in amazement. Sometimes I say, "I know, but who cares? It's a *great* story!" Other times I am genuinely perplexed. "It's not?" I say then. "But I was so sure it was."

The reason for my varying responses is simple. Sometimes I know I am exaggerating, deliberately choosing to use hyperbole or dramatization to make the storytelling experience sing. Other times I am so deeply immersed in the sensations of the story that I actually begin to believe my own embroideries. Christine, who told the story of the Christmas basket in chapter three, purposely used hyperbole to snare her child's attention when she added the part about the dog's bark freezing in midair. Hyperbole is fun, especially when it is as extreme as Christine's, and it in no way sullies the basic truth of the story. But what about the times when I get so caught up in my stories that I do not even realize how much I am exaggerating or when I deliberately change a fact or two to make the story better? What is that all about? And more importantly, does it obscure or invalidate a sacred story?

According to storytelling experts Alida Gersie and Nancy King, our embellishments put our individual stamp on a story and reflect our deepest longings and needs, as well as our sense of possibility. In other words, when we exaggerate, we project onto the story the most intimate and revealing *truths about ourselves.* It is important to make it clear, however, that there is a significant difference between storytelling and equivocating. If I tell a story to make myself look more heroic that I actually was or if I change the facts so that someone is hurt, then I am no longer telling a story, but a lie. Any time the essential truth of a story is misrepresented, we cross the line. What Gersie and King are referring to, as every good storyteller knows, is the process of telling the story in such a way as to give it greater urgency and interest.[3] At the same time, the storyteller ministers to the parts of herself that cry out to be heard. Let me share a perfect example.

During the waning days of March 1975, Eric and I lived on the raw edge of emotion, glued to the TV watching helplessly as the government of South Vietnam crumbled like clods of dry earth before our eyes. The previous year we had applied to adopt a Vietnamese child and had been lending support to an orphanage run by a Roman Catholic nun ever since. As the drama escalated on the screen, so did our fear that Sister and the children would be killed as communist forces from Hanoi moved in from the north and laid claim to Saigon. Just when it appeared that all hope had been spent, President Ford announced plans for a massive airlift of babies and children to the United States. Though we did not dare breathe easily, we comforted ourselves with the thought that the

U.S. government had the capability to evacuate large numbers of kids. Surely, we told each other, it would be all right.

It wasn't.

On April 4, a U.S. Air Force C-58 cargo jet carrying the first airlift of children crashed shortly after taking off from Tan Son Nhut air base, killing approximately 100 of the 243 babies and children on board and injuring many more. As workmen milled around me installing new cabinets in my kitchen, I stood against the wall, clutching the phone and screaming in horror.

Two days later I turned twenty-five. The first thought I had when I woke up on the morning of my birthday was, *My baby's coming home today.* There was no earthly reason to think such a thing. Though our name had been near the top of the list before the political situation became so desperate, we had not as yet been assigned a child, so there was little chance that one of the hundreds of children brought to the United States in the two days since the crash would be ours. Many were the children of American servicemen, many more were already in the process of adoption. Besides, our paperwork was caught in a hopeless bottleneck in Columbus. And yet the thought persisted. *My baby's coming home today.*

"I wish you wouldn't do this," Eric said, at least fifty times throughout the course of the day. "I think you're setting yourself up for a fall." But all day long I continued to wait expectantly for the phone to ring. For the first time since the beginning of the fall of Saigon, I felt buoyant. I was so sure that my baby would be arriving soon that I actually began making plans to buy the necessary baby gear. But by midnight when the phone remained painfully silent, even I finally had to admit I had been mistaken. Three weeks later, instead of a baby, we got a family of eight refugees.

To say that I was disappointed is an understatement. Disappointment is but a shadow of the deep disillusionment I felt as I busied myself with the enormous process of settling Ha Thuc and his family. The feeling had been so strong, so persistent, so *sure*, it seemed incomprehensible that it had also been dead wrong. But then one day in early June I picked up the phone and heard such startling, unexpected news I could barely squeak out a reply. The adoption agency had found us a two-month-old baby girl from Korea! In less than an hour we were sitting in the social worker's office in Akron holding an official-looking document to which was attached a small black-and-white snapshot of a tiny baby peering out from the folds of a blanket. At exactly the same moment that I glanced at the photo, her date of birth jumped out at me in 3-D like the image in a Magic Eye picture.

There are two ways to tell the rest of the story—the way I *like* to tell it and honestly believe to be the truth, and the way it actually happened. Let's go with what actually happened. The date of birth listed on the document said April 2, 1975, which of course, is four days before I woke up with that overwhelming sense of certainty. *But*—and this is the crucial part—next to the date was typed the magic word *estimated.* Moira had been found without a birth certificate or any other form of identity and was brought to the Holt adoption agency in Seoul, South Korea, on May 2. The attending physician guessed her to be a month old. "They're pretty accurate with babies as young as this one," the social worker informed us. "He's not off by more than a few days either way."

A few days either way. Those were the words I needed to hear. In my heart I will always believe that my feeling of certainty and her date of birth coincided. Perhaps it has less to do with reality than it does with my need to believe it—I do not know. The point is that the embroidery work we do on our stories stems from the deepest needs and yearnings of the heart.

Truth and Myth

No discussion of storytelling and truth is complete without a look at myth, a form that human beings have used to tell stories about the sacred for millenniums. Unfortunately, the word *myth* makes some people extremely nervous. "It's just a myth," they say disparagingly, as though myth has no more value than yesterday's junk mail. Some even go so far as to dismiss story in exactly the same way. "Oh, that's not true," they say confidently, "it's just a story." Which is about like saying that a B-52 is "just" a bomber!

The best definition I have ever heard of myth was offered by an

Episcopalian Jungian psychologist and author from California named Robert Johnson. He said, "A myth is something that's true on the inside, but not on the outside."[4] Myths help us make sense of the world. They also show us the significance of our existence. Whether we realize it or not, every family lives out its own personal myth in the sense that each family patterns its life around a certain set of beliefs, 90 percent of which may remain below the surface of consciousness. One family I spoke with cherished the myth that life is a continuous beach party. At first glance this would seem almost delusional. Their mother had suffered from alcoholism for many years before dying of breast cancer in her fifties; the oldest son had run into difficulties with the law; another child suffers from mental illness; and two of the siblings are estranged from one another. Yet each member persists in seeing the family as perpetually basking in the sun!

"We grew up in an ocean-front home where money was something you took for granted," says Deborah, the youngest child. "My parents entertained constantly, as did we kids. People were constantly coming and going, and there was always a lot of laughter and good times. Even when the world was whirling off its axis, we partied on. It's how we survived, I guess. We told ourselves that we were golden people, and we believed it. To those who don't know us well, it might seem like we've lost our grip on reality. But if we've survived a lot of hard knocks, then we've had a pretty great time doing it."

The late psychotherapist Rollo May, a graduate of New York's Union Theological Seminary, pointed out that we badly need myth in our lives to perform at least four vital functions. First, myth tells us who we are and where we come from. Second, it makes it possible for us to enjoy a sense of community. The passionate loyalties we develop to our families, our alma maters and even our favorite basketball teams arise from myth. Third, myth provides a foundation for our moral values. And fourth, it helps us to deal with the mystery of creation—not only of the world but also of the dawning of art and ideas.[5] Whether or not the beach-party myth is one we would choose to fashion for our own families, it provides all four of these benefits to the family that wrote it. Their myth is the glue that holds their family framework together. Even though it fails to overtly address the subject of God and spirituality, it speaks eloquently to the family's beliefs about it, as myths always do. Compare it to a very different kind of family myth told to me by professional storyteller Cindy Guthrie.

As Cindy tells the story, she and her husband were taking a walk around their neighborhood when they chanced upon a large St. Bernard dog that had been injured and was unable to walk. The city dog warden was already on the scene, preparing to take the dog to the pound, when Cindy's husband, an Episcopal priest, suddenly heard the dog whisper, "My God, my God, why hast thou forsaken me? . . . I am poured out like water, and all my bones are out of joint" (Psalm 22:1, 14).

At this point there was nothing else they could do, Cindy says, but negotiate with the warden for permission to take responsibility for the animal. Next they went to a nearby veterinarian, who told them to take it home and keep a close watch over it for the next three days to determine whether or not its back was broken. Once they got it home, the dog lay virtually inert on the kitchen floor. Cindy's husband went next door to the church and returned a few minutes later, garbed in his clerical robes and carrying a very old Roman Catholic Book of Blessings from which he read a prayer for animals. As soon as he finished the impromptu service, the dog stood up, healed. They named him Bosco after Saint John Bosco, an Italian priest who spent his life caring for homeless boys. Today, a decade later, Bosco the miracle dog continues to grace their lives.

When we look at the story of Bosco in light of Rollo May's four criteria, we begin to understand the workings of myth and why we so desperately need it to shape our family's identity. The story, which is built around the very common experience of finding and caring for a stray animal, can easily be told with an emphasis on historical accuracy and still be a valid and interesting story. But when the storyteller infuses it with her own imagination, she makes it much more intensely personal because she shares her vulnerability, faith, wit and wisdom, all parts of her deepest self. The story also forges several connections: between the teller and her family, between the teller and anyone who loves animals or has ever shared the experience of keeping vigil over the sick, and between the teller and the entire community of believers. Though its biblical and ecclesiastical references are Christian, the essential truth that the story conveys is universal to anyone who believes in the sublime magnificence of the Creator.

What's more, the story leaves little question about the moral values of the author. It speaks of the need to take responsibility for the least of God's creatures, about inconveniencing oneself for a greater good and about belief in God's willingness to heal. It also says in a memorable and entertaining way that God listens to even the humblest prayers, including the anguished cries of a wounded dog. The story speaks to the subject of creation for the simple reason that it is itself a creative act. It also tells the listener that health and hope can be created out of pain and suffering when a strong, immediate faith expresses itself through prayer and ritual. In light of all that, does it really matter whether or not the dog actually whispered Psalm 22?

And yet there are times when you stand back in awe of events exactly as they occurred. You know intuitively that, at least in this instance, embellishment would be sacrilege. The need for the story to accurately reflect the awesome power of God becomes so essential that you would rather risk a milder reaction from the audience than tamper with a single detail. Kathryn, whom we met in the last chapter, feels precisely this way when she shares stories of the many marvelous things that have happened since the death of her son Mac in the bicycle accident.

One evening she and her family went out to dinner at Mac's favorite Chinese restaurant. Although it was the first time they had been there since the tragedy, it felt right and welcoming somehow, almost as though Mac had joined them at the table. Before long everyone was relaxed, laughing, reminiscing and enjoying each other's company. Just as the waiter brought their entrees, a piano player launched into a selection of easy-listening tunes, something that had never before happened in all the times they had patronized the restaurant. One of his first numbers was Beethoven's "Für Elise."

At the sound of the familiar melody, Kathryn felt a tingle of delight. It was a song she loved so much that she had named her daughter Heather Elise. To hear it played in so improbable a setting seemed one more blessing in an evening filled with them, as she had worried for a long time that Heather felt lost and abandoned in the midst of so much sorrow. "That song is like a hug to her," she says.

As the last notes died away, delight turned to astonishment as the piano player immediately swung into a bouncy Scott Joplin number. It was not Mac's early-morning favorite, "The Entertainer," but it was so evocative of him that it almost took her breath away. "What are the odds of classical music and ragtime being played back to back in a Chinese restaurant?" she asks, laughing.

As I listen, my storyteller's mind immediately latches onto the obvious. "Don't you ever feel a tiny bit tempted to change the second song to 'The Entertainer'?" I ask.

Her response is immediate. "Never. Since Mac's death God has sent me so many gifts that I feel an obligation to be as accurate as possible in reporting them. What happened at the restaurant isn't even the most astounding thing I've experienced, but even the small stories have to be right."

Cindy's telling her story as myth and Kathryn's focusing on literal truth both go back to the need for authenticity. No one else shares your exact experience of the sacred, so no one else can tell you how to tell your stories. As you become more experienced with the storytelling process, you begin to notice a strong correlation between storytelling and prayer. Not only does storytelling become a form of prayer itself, but it also derives from the *experience* of prayer. Nowhere are we more genuine than in our attempt to communicate with the divine.

Storytelling on Our Knees

"Prayer is conversation," says author Elizabeth Cody Newenhuyse. "It's telling God our stories. As our lives unfold, we bring each new story to God as though it's news to him. And God is very indulgent, even when we're dealing with the same issues over and over in different guises."[6]

The stories we bring to the feet of God are most private and personal, stories that are sometimes so fragile that to speak of them openly to others before we are ready, or to allow them to be heard by the wrong ears, would risk their (and perhaps even at times our own) disintegration. But it is this very fragility that teaches us what it means to be authentic. From the experience of talking to God with the vulnerable language of the heart we learn to tell our stories to the most important people in our lives with the same guilelessness.

Of course prayer consists of much more than talking. Meditative prayer, the experience of sitting in silence with an empty mind and an open heart, teaches us much about storytelling as well. From it we learn the humble art of listening. We tell our stories to God and wait for a reply, just as we tell our stories to others and wait in a spirit of expectancy for them to tell us theirs. As Sam Keen and Anne Valley Fox so beautifully put it in their book *Your Mythic Journey: Finding Meaning in Your Life Through Writing and Storytelling,* "Your own stories will hollow you out so you can listen to the stories of others, as common and unique as your own. Through story we overcome our loneliness, develop compassion and create community."

Before we can listen wholeheartedly and nonjudgmentally to the stories of others, it is necessary to experience what it means to be heard. I can think of no better way than by being silent and listening to what George Fox, the founder of the Quakers, called "the still, small voice" within. Meditative prayer leads us to answer the call of Psalm 46:10: "Be still, and know that I am God." As we begin to realize that God gives undivided attention to each of us *whenever we ask for it,* we begin at last to understand what it means to bestow the gift of complete attention on others as they tell their own stories.

Contemplative prayer also has much to teach us about storytelling. As we read the Word of God or the spiritual writings of other teachers, we need time and silence to assimilate what we have learned. Reading the story of Jesus' calming the storm the night he and his disciples went out together in a fishing boat may increase our intellectual understanding of the Bible, but until it engages our senses and emotions, it does little to show us what the story means to our lives. The path to insight is experiential. In other words, if you want to understand the fear, you have to get out on the water! It's the same with the stories you share in your family. Until you have felt the salt spray and have heard the cacophony of jumbled, confusing languages shouting in voices that soar with elation, it is pretty tough to understand and care how your grandmother felt when she first saw the Statue of Liberty. And it is nearly impossible to make the link between that experience and the time you stood at the rim of the Grand Canyon and found yourself so overwhelmed that the words of poet Edna St. Vincent Millay sprang to your lips like a prayer, "Oh world, I cannot hold thee close enough."[7]

I think I must have been about seven years old when I first heard the story of Jesus calming the storm, but it was not until fairly recently that I had an "Aha!" experience with it. One day it suddenly occurred to me that the disciples actually brought the storm inside the boat—into the place where God resides—just as I do when I allow my fears to overshadow my faith. From that point on, the boat (I see it as weathered, its blue paint scarred and worn from the pounding of the waves and the lick of salt air) has become a personal metaphor for "the peace of God that passes all understanding." Whenever I feel myself spinning off into a panic, I visualize myself inside the dark, quiet safety of the boat, gazing out at the thunderous tumult with detached fascination.

Bill Martin Jr., author and editor of the Sounds of Language reading series, says that each person maintains a "linguistic storehouse" into which he deposits the stories, poems, words and phrases that remain available to him throughout his life. Before a story can be meaningful enough to be deposited, it must first strike a resonant note. Very often it takes much repetition and contemplation to make that happen, which is why storytelling and ritual go hand in hand.[9]

The most profound example of ritualistic storytelling, of course, is the Eucharist. As the bread is broken and the ancient words are intoned, the story of the Last Supper becomes *our* story, acted out as though for the very first time—even as it reminds us of our place in the continuum.

"On the night before he died for us, our Lord Jesus Christ took bread; and when he had given thanks to you, he broke it, and gave it to his disciples, and said, 'Take, eat: This is my Body, which is given for you. Do this for the remembrance of me.'"[10] More than a thousand times those words have washed over me—in the church of my childhood, in my beautiful little neighborhood church, in a dingy, faded inner-city church in Cleveland, in the cavernous Cathedral of St. John the Divine in New York, in a tiny country parish in Ireland, in Lake Placid and Chautauqua and Tucson and Toronto. Each time, the imprint they left on my soul grew deeper. Sometimes I was so busy daydreaming about Saturday night's dance or worrying about whether or not I had turned the iron off that I barely heard the words. And yet they quietly went about the business of branding me, of making themselves a part of my linguistic storehouse.

As you begin the adventure of seeking God at the fireside through your family stories, do not worry about whether everybody is getting the "right" message. Concentrate instead on bringing to your stories love, laughter and childlike wonder. The message will take care of itself. God, after all, lives in the details. And so do you.

Things to Talk About

1. How do you feel about coincidences? Explore some of your own stories that seem almost too amazing to be true. What do they tell you about God?

2. Think about the ways you "embroider" the stories you tell. What do these embellishments reveal about you?

3. How do you react to the word *myth*? What is your family's myth and why do you think it came to be written? In what ways is it the glue that holds your family's framework together? Relate it to Rollo May's four functions of myth.

5. Do stories foster your spiritual life? In what ways? How do you relate storytelling and prayer?

Things to Do Right Now

1. Write a favorite family story as a myth. Tell it to your family and talk about what the myth says about your family's framework. Better yet, write a family myth together.

Six

Stopping at the Troll Bridge
Children Telling Stories

A̲N INFECTIOUS LITTLE GIGGLE BROUGHT ME BACK FROM THE MEDITER-
ranean with a jolt. I sat up and blinked, slightly disoriented to find
myself lying on a patchwork quilt spread out on a bumpy hillside in
Ohio. The giggler, wearing only a diaper, cavorted through the
gathering gloom, dancing to *Bolero* and waving a nursing bottle of
apple juice by its nipple. Clunk! The plastic bottle thumped her
father's bald head. For the space of a second she looked surprised,
and then she let out a deep, rumbling belly laugh.

Inveterate baby gazers, Eric and I immediately forgot the concert
and watched, entranced, as she toddled over to a neighboring blanket,
pointed back at her father with a tiny forefinger and chortled, "Bottle.
Daddy. Head. Ow-w-w! Funny!"

"She told a story!" we exclaimed simultaneously.

And indeed she had. At twenty months, Alexandra was already
translating experience into story. Primitive though it was, her
microstory had a beginning, a middle and an end. What's more, it
conveyed her feelings about an event in her life that she considered

significant, and she invited her listeners to share in the experience. Psychologists report that by age three most children are capable of telling a complete story and by five have even developed their own unique storytelling style. By eight most are capable of relating complex events, as any parent who has ever sat through the entire convoluted plot of a movie can attest!

Telling family stories to children is like drawing them a treasure map; allowing them to tell their own is like watching while they dig up the jewels. When kids tell stories to a supportive audience, they grow in self-confidence, learn to express their feelings, develop problem-solving skills, form a point of view and acquire a solid sense of themselves, both as individuals and as members of a larger community. According to educational psychologist Jane M. Healy, children who are poor conversationalists very likely carry on poor internal dialogues with themselves. You may not consider the ability to talk engagingly to yourself a significant accomplishment, but research has proven that self-talk is essential for developing reading comprehension skills, motivation and creativity. In a world she views as becoming increasingly nonverbal, thanks to passive activities such as video games and computers, Healy fears that the upcoming generation is losing its ability to communicate, a process that ideally begins in the home. "Brains grow around what they do and what they are exposed to," Healy says. "More and more, children are coming into our schools without the skills to communicate with their peers, much less with adults."

Kids who are encouraged to tell stories learn to relate to adults in a meaningful way, think creatively and get a jump-start on literacy. Susan Engel, author of *The Stories Children Tell: Making Sense of the Narratives of Childhood,* calls storytelling "the most important aspect of literary development in children." It is important to read to children of all ages, Engel says, but in order for little ones to "leap into literacy," they must be encouraged to tell their own stories to a listening audience. Stories help children expand their vocabularies and begin to use words to paint images that are often dazzlingly sophisticated.[1]

One mother rifled through a desk drawer, produced an old journal that she had kept during her son's second year and read me an entry dated February 22, 1990: "Travis told me a story today. He said, 'Once upon a time, a long time ago, we went for a walk and the stars were white ridges in the sky.'" Another mother commented that on opening the front door to greet an unexpected snowfall, her five-year-old mentally challenged daughter exclaimed, "That snow looks like a wrinkled sheet." The ability to form pictures in the mind helps kids become better readers and better mathematicians.

Diana Budney teaches sixth grade at Lodi Elementary School in Lodi, Ohio. She is a natural storyteller who makes strong use of story as an educational tool in the classroom. She reports that during her fifteen-year career approximately 30 to 40 percent of the children she has taught have had no stories at their disposal other than the ones they have seen on TV. When asked to write or tell about a family story in the classroom, these kids look at her blankly, having no idea how to begin. It does not take them long to realize that before they can effectively tell their own stories, they first have to absorb other people's in order to familiarize themselves with the special language and rhythm of story. So they hang around her on the playground begging for stories to fill up the empty well. Once they have been exposed to the power of story, Budney says, their thirst for it is almost unquenchable.

Professional storyteller Cindy Guthrie agrees. A number of years ago she and a friend from her local storytelling group told stories to the residents of a teen runaway shelter. Even under ideal circumstances, telling stories to teens is a tough gig, as peer pressure practically ensures the need for them to project an "I am too totally cool for this stuff" image. Telling stories to streetwise kids who have piled up enough negative experiences to build an impenetrable wall around their emotions can feel a lot like trying to hack through an iron bar with a plastic knife. But amazingly enough, the kids inhaled the stories like oxygen—especially the boys. It wasn't that the girls didn't want stories, Guthrie says. But they could not relate to strong heroines who exhibited goals, determination, strength and courage. Already at twelve and thirteen years of age, they yearned to hear Cinderella stories of strong, dashing princes charging in on white steeds and sweeping the poor misbegotten "heroines" off to happily-ever-after land.

Because these girls had never been exposed to stories of family heroines and had never been empowered to tell their own stories, they saw themselves as passive bystanders to whom bad things "just happen." I could not help but contrast them with the fifth-grader who proudly told me the story of her great-grandmother from Pittsburgh who had been one of the first librarians hired during the early part of the nineteenth century, when Andrew Carnegie contributed vast sums of money to open lending libraries in the United States. "She hadn't even been to college," Tiffany said, "but she studied like crazy and took a very hard test and passed it. The women in my family are all really smart. My grandma was a teacher and so is my mom. I'm going to be a marine biologist myself."

Clearly, her family's stories, combined with her own considerable storytelling abilities, have given this child a strong vision of her future self. During the hour we spent together, she told me at least a dozen tales and gave me a decisive, unsolicited opinion about each of them. Unlike adults, children generally do not find it necessary to interpret the stories they tell, but Tiffany may have been the exception. I was free to think what I liked about any of them, but she wanted there to be no mistake about what *she* thought! Tiffany also confirmed my suspicions that she had been encouraged to tell stories from an early age.

Researchers have found that children tell stories in two distinct areas of their lives: in interactions with others and during symbolic play. These stories, especially the ones told during play, provide a magnifying lens through which parents and teachers can view the complex interior world of childhood. One mother mentioned that for weeks after her daughter's hospitalization for a tonsillectomy, she reenacted the surgery daily with her dolls, but only when she thought no one else was listening.

"It was fascinating," Marsha says. "She'd put Barbie in the doll bed and jab her with a toothpick, and Barbie, of course, would cry. Then she'd say, 'Don't cry, Barbie. You're going to sleep pretty soon, and when you wake up it will be all over.' At this point Ken would come in and stick a plastic bowl over Barbie's face, and she'd kick her legs and scream no-no with such ferocity it would absolutely stop your heart. To this, Ken would say in a comforting voice, 'Easy now, Barbie. Easy.' But what absolutely held me mesmerized was the way she told Barbie the story of what it was like to be under anesthesia. It was like Alice falling down the rabbit hole. I don't know how much is true and how much is imagined, but it made me realize just how traumatic an experience surgery had been for her. Before, whenever I'd try to talk with her about it, she'd either start acting silly or get preoccupied with something else. I actually thought she hadn't considered it a big deal."

Researchers have found that 70 percent of all the stories children tell are personal experiences. Whether they tell stories in anticipation of an event or in summation of it, children use stories, just as adults do, to come to grips with their emotions. Very often the events children relate can seem so simplistic that parents make the mistake of brushing them off as unimportant. But to the child they are fascinating puzzles, the pieces of which must be carefully reassembled to give closure to the day or to the event itself. Sometimes these stories can be highly symbolic. Though the child uses metaphor unconsciously, it is a tool that can help him confront scary issues and feelings more comfortably than meeting them head-on.

In the days after a fire burned his family's home to the ground, a three-year-old boy endlessly repeated the story of how his father's computer had been destroyed. Over and over, with considerable animation and excitement, he would say, "Daddy's 'puter is all gone. The fire burned it up and now it's gone *forever!*"

His teacher, Laurie, says that at first she was surprised to hear him focus on an item that wasn't even his, especially in light of the fact that he had lost all his clothes and toys, and even his bedroom. But after hearing the story more than half a dozen times in a single day, she began to realize that Bobby saw the computer as his father's most valuable possession. As such, it represented everything that is orderly, important and dependable in the world. Even though he seemed to be telling the story of the fire as a great adventure, she was sensitive enough to see that the loss of this symbol of security had deeply frightened him. By cracking the symbolic code, she was able to help him resolve a confusing array of feelings.

As the children of Bosnia struggle with the aftermath of a war that cost more than two thousand of them their parents, siblings and homes, psychologists are likewise turning to the power of story to help them deal with overwhelming feelings of grief, loss and fear. At the SOS Kinderdorf Center in Sarajevo, children learn to tell "the never-ending story" that plays in their heads like a horror movie that keeps rewinding with a fiendish will of its own. Beginning with the sentence "once there was a family and then the war came," the children draw six pictures depicting what happened in its aftermath. The drawings of people, burning homes, guns, tanks and airplanes help them form the words to tell what happened when the war robbed them of their childhoods.[2]

Fantasia
When very small children tell a story, it is not uncommon for them to shift from reality to fantasy. One young mother I spoke with reported this phenomenon when she was giving her three-year-old son a dose of cold medicine. After he had swallowed the spoonful of thick syrup and licked the spoon, he looked up at her and said, "When you were a little girl, you were very sick and I knew you were going to be my mommy, so I came down from heaven like an angel with my umbrella and fed you Dimetapp. That makes me a hero, doesn't it?" Carla says she knew at once that it was an amalgamation of a story she had told him about her childhood bout with pneumonia, the story of Mary Poppins he watched on video, the story of the angel Gabriel visiting Mary that they had just read in a children's Bible story book, and the actual experience of taking medicine in the here and now, along with a smattering of *Mighty Morphin Power Rangers,* his favorite TV show. "It was amazing how all those diverse stories came together for him that way," she says. "I was awed by how much he'd taken in and how his mind was sorting through it all."

Older kids are much less likely to employ fantasy in their stories, but to very young children the line between what is real and what is fictive can be as hazy as a San Francisco morning. Small children are also less inhibited, freer to play with the bounty of the imagination than older kids, who begin to feel self-conscious and afraid to seem "babyish." For many this creative play produces an imaginary friend. About a fourth of the people I spoke with reported either having had such a friend themselves or experiencing the phenomenon with their own children. Author Elizabeth Cody Newenhuyse speaks with warmth about the two imaginary friends she had as a child: a little girl she named Lorraine Hadley and Lorraine's friend, Della. Looking back at the hours of creative interplay with these characters and how they inspired her to begin writing stories, she says that she is deeply grateful to have had parents wise enough to value the life of the imagination. Too often parents who are uncomfortable with creativity want to rush in and squelch flights of fancy rather than allowing them to enrich the life of the entire family. "My son had an imaginary friend named Journey," one father told me. "It drove me nuts. I'd sit down on the couch and he'd scream that I was sitting on Journey's foot or something. Finally, I put a stop to it. It seems to me that kids need to know the difference between what's real and what's not."

The fear that children will fail to distinguish between reality and fantasy keeps many parents from allowing their children's imaginary friends into the family story bag. Others worry that it may encourage lying. But when our younger daughter, Caitie, produced an imaginary friend at age three, she launched us all on an incredible joy ride that nine years later remains a treasured part of our family lore. She also taught us in a poignant way that when the products of the imagination are no longer needed, they get packed away in a dusty corner of the attic right along with the Easy Bake ovens and the G.I. Joes.

Caitie's imaginary friend had the rather unfortunate name Honky, but we quickly discovered that it came from the Honkers (two of the fuzzy monsters on *Sesame Street*) and the geese that annually take up residence at the lake behind our house. I cannot recall exactly when Honky arrived in our lives, but I do know that Eric and I were instantly charmed. We would be sitting in the family room on a Friday night watching TV and Caitie would suddenly spring up, fling open the door, and cry with unabashed joy, "Honky! You're here!" At this point everybody would say, "Hi, Honk. Glad you could make it. Want some pizza?" Like most small children, Caitie's internal radar quickly picked up on the fact that she had found an appreciative audience, so it wasn't long before several other characters appeared on the scene as well—Honky's parents, Cindy and Coco, and her younger sisters, Pinky and Kiwi. They lived, she told us solemnly, in Salt Lake City. "But that's impossible," Moira, who was twelve then, told her. "That's in Utah." Moira even showed her on the map how far Utah was from Ohio, but Caitie wasn't buying it.

"They can get here," she said firmly. End of discussion.

Whenever I think of Caitie's imaginary friend, one memory stands out. We have told the story so many times that when it comes time to dump out the contents of the family story bag for one final look, it will definitely be among the most well-worn. One day when Caitie was four, she came running into the house crying because a friend was having a birthday party and had not invited her, even though the friend had attended Caitie's party six months ago. "They're going to have a swimming party at the pool," she sobbed, "and they say I can't go because I'm too little."

Though Caitie was a year younger and a head shorter than her friend, I suspected (and Caitie knew) that neither age nor size had anything to do with the lack of invitation. Like most moms, I had to swallow an immediate surge of righteous indignation, wipe the tear-stained little face in front of me and figure out a way to salvage what was left of my child's self-esteem. Almost instantly, I thought of Honky. "Hey, you know what?" I said brightly. "It would have been fun to go to the party, but I'm not sure you would have had time anyway. Coco told me that today's Honky's birthday, so I figure we'd better do something about it. Don't you think we need to get a party of our own going here?"

For a second she looked at me in amazement. Then she sniffed loudly and nodded. "Yes, I do," she said, her voice so serious I had to swallow a lump in my throat the size of a boulder. Since Eric was out of town and Moira was at a sleepover at a friend's house, Caitie and I celebrated Honky's birthday by ourselves that evening. She planned the menu (cabbage rolls and chocolate cake), and we spent the afternoon happily smearing tomato sauce and cocoa around the kitchen. Fortunately, Honky's age and the number of linty birthday candles we scrounged out of the junk drawer matched perfectly—five. We set the table in the dining room with the best china, used the leftover teddy bear napkins from Caitie's own party, sang "Happy Birthday" and blew out the candles.

As I tucked Caitie (and Honky) into bed that night, I knew we had experienced something profound and sacred. Not long ago I asked Caitie to name her favorite family story. Without a second's hesitation she replied, "The one about Honky's birthday party because it's so funny."

Honky and her family remained in our lives for several more years. One day when Caitie was seven, she came into my office, sat down on the couch and told me she needed to tell me something important. The earnestness in her voice snagged my attention immediately. "Mom, I don't want you to feel bad or anything," she said. "But I have to tell you something about Honky."

"What's that?" I asked, ready to jump into the game.

"Honky's not real. I made her up."

In that instant I knew that Caitie's imaginary family would not be visiting us anymore and also knew there was nothing I could do to resurrect it. Part of me felt sad to part with the frivolity it had brought us, but another part rejoiced to see her make the decision to move into another stage of maturation. Actually, I think that she had long ago made the differentiation *for herself* between the things she creates and the things that are concrete, but had kept the game going for the sheer delight of it. None of us will ever forget Caitie's fictitious family, but more than that, we'll never forget the way a small child's imagination had the power to create a memory we all treasure, a memory that could have arisen only from *our* family.

Another family I spoke with cherishes a memory that clearly illustrates how children's minds sometimes make enchanting detours into the world of fantasy, even when they attempt to tell the story of an actual event. A few summers ago Connie and her husband asked their four-year-old daughter, Tara, to tell Grandma about their summer vacation. "We-e-e-ll," Tara said, drawing the word out dramatically, "we drove and drove and drove and finally we came to the troll bridge . . ."

"What kind of bridge?" Connie interrupted.

"The troll bridge," Tara replied patiently. "You know—where you have to pay money to drive on the road. But it was daytime, so there weren't any trolls around. There was only a lady in a little glass house." She leaned confidentially toward her grandmother and whispered, "But she looked kind of mean. I think she was the boss of the trolls!"

Every summer since, Connie's family has been sure to stop at the "troll bridge." "It's one of those funny things that will live forever in our family," she says. "Even my sixteen-year-old son calls a toll booth a troll bridge!"

Researchers have found that small children begin to attain storytelling skills by telling stories along with an adult, a process called conarrating. Many stories written for children contain repetitive lines, such as the little gingerbread boy's famous "Run, run, as fast as you can, but you can't catch me, I'm the gingerbread man!" This technique allows the child to both anticipate and engage in the action. Diana Budney says that parents can foster storytelling skills by adapting fictive stories to family events and employing repetition to encourage the child to help tell the story. By blending fantasy with facts about the child's life, even parents who are not born storytellers can introduce their children to the art of creative narrative.

Budney discovered this technique the hard way when the wheel of her family's pop-up camper fell off in Connecticut while they were touring the New England coastline. During the eleven and a half hours it took to make the repair, she and her two-year-old son read every picture book they had packed at least six times each and colored every picture in his coloring book. Ordinarily they would have rented a hotel room, but a set of decorative refrigerator magnets they had bought as a gift had demagnetized all their credit cards, so they needed to conserve cash. Desperate, Budney turned to storytelling.

Of all the stories she told that day, the one that continues to live on in family history is the personalized version of "The Three Little Pigs." Using her son's name and the names of his cousins for the pigs, she had them building their houses out of "wicker like Grandma's," logs "like at the Ponderosa" and bricks like the ones used by her father, a housing contractor. When the fox tried to huff and puff and blow the brick house down, he was unsuccessful because "nothing bad can happen to the houses Grandpa builds!" A classic children's story became a tender tale about her child's relationship with his grandfather. When he got home, her son told the story to his grandpa. Later it was told with different names to other family children, and it continues to be passed along to this day.

Fantasy can also be adapted to family stories by establishing family storytelling rituals. Every Christmas Budney writes a holiday mystery story and sends clues to each of her thirty-two nieces and nephews. On Christmas Eve the entire extended family gathers for a huge breakfast. All of the kids, from preschoolers to teens, get twenty-five minutes to share what they know about the story and work together to crack the case. This year's story focused on a battalion of G.I. Joe commandos who took over the Power Rangers' factory. Though the Christmas mysteries themselves are always fictitious and rarely contain personalized details, the ritual itself has become rich fodder for family stories. The stories teach problem-solving skills, encourage cooperation and forge a sense of family unity. But most importantly, they create lasting memories—one of the major goals of storytelling.

The Tried and True

As a parent, you naturally want your children to remember the special, fleeting moments of childhood and to cherish the brief time you share together under one roof. So many times I have heard my own kids say, "I'm not sure whether I actually remember this, or if it's just that I heard the story so often, but one time . . ." Factual stories play an enormous role in your child's development because they give him the gift of his own childhood as seen through both his own eyes and the eyes of those who love him. By encouraging your child to tell you simple stories of what happened at Grandma's house or what he did at school, and by shaping family happenings into the stories that you tell to him, you endow the simple events of childhood with value and meaning and help him remember them. Eventually each day's little stories will flow into pools—the pool of nursery school, the pool of summer, the pool of camp. All he needs to dip into any one of them is a fragmentary reminder. A few lines of the song "Little Bunny Foo-Foo," the smell of craft glue, the mention of Jello-O Jigglers, and he is right back in Mrs. Bennett's preschool class in the church basement.

Linda, the mom we met in a previous chapter who works as a mentor to other parents through her church, told me that when her children were small, they often stayed overnight at their grandparents' house. Each time they came home after a sleepover, she made it a point to ask them what they had done. Although the stories were usually pretty predictable, she always reacted as though hearing them for the first time. Today one of their favorite memories of childhood is staying overnight with Grammy and Papaw, watching Saturday-morning cartoons in their pajamas and eating pancakes and supermarket syrup. It may not be the stuff of epics, but it is definitely the stuff of memories.

A grandmother I spoke with, another natural storyteller, shared how she had been able to take a tiny event from her grandson's life and connect it with family history to create a very special Christmas memory. It captured a piece of his past, showed him his own special place in the family continuum and gave him a tangible vehicle through which to tell the story himself. One holiday season Timmy announced to his parents that this year he wanted them to buy a live, balled Christmas tree that could be planted in the yard when Christmas was over. Pat, his grandmother, was amazed at the news because Timmy had inadvertently tapped into an almost-forgotten family tradition.

As a child growing up during the war years, she had once planted her own Christmas tree. It still stands, even though the family has not lived in the house for many years. Years later, one of her own children had also planted a Christmas tree, and that tree had grown so large that it almost completely filled the space between her house and the one next door. And now Timmy wanted to plant a tree too. As a gift, Pat wrote and illustrated for him the simple story of the three trees and bound it into a book. Because he has both read and told the story countless times, it will undoubtedly follow him into adulthood and may even inspire him to someday dig a deep hole and plant a sturdy spruce with a child or grandchild of his own.

As a parent or a grandparent, you exert considerable influence over how family stories are remembered and told. Phil, a father of two teenagers, reminded me of this when he commented, "I always tell my children that the relationship they have with each other is one of the most important they will ever know because someday, after their mother and I are gone, they will be each other's only link to childhood."

We were talking about how family stories foster lasting memories. Phil was telling me that his mother had taken every opportunity to tell stories of special moments shared by him and his siblings in a way that encouraged them to want to tell them as well. He laughed as he recalled a favorite that he and his sister still enjoy, thirty years after it happened. When Kathleen was eight and Phil five, Kathleen made her First Communion. She wore the white dress and veil that was required of her by the Roman Catholic Church. Phil took one look at his favorite sister coming down the stairs in the frilly outfit and burst into a storm of noisy tears, convinced that she was getting married and leaving the family home forever. "Now *there's* a story you could easily come to hate!" he recalled. "But, thanks to my mom, it's one that brings back warm memories. In fact, when Kathleen got married twenty years later, I used it as the centerpiece of the toast I gave at her wedding reception."

The key to the story's success, he emphasized, is focus. Instead of embarrassing him for not understanding what was happening, his wise mother shifted the emphasis onto the special bond between him and his sister and encouraged them to be part of the retelling. Even though his aunts, uncles and grandparents enjoyed a laugh when the story was told to the extended family the afternoon of the First Communion party, he came away feeling like a hero. He also remembers that his mother made a ceremony of cutting the cake and giving both him and Kathleen prime pieces cut from the center and topped with the biggest icing roses.

"We were made to feel special for caring about each other so much," he explained. "But that wasn't even the whole thing. My mother molded that incident like a piece of clay so that it belonged to the two of us and only to us. It's a valuable lesson about family stories that has stuck with me for a lifetime. My wife and I vowed from the start to make certain that our family stories have a similarly civilizing effect on our kids."

Taming the Wildebeest

Phil's choice of the word *civilizing* brought me up short. It made me think of family stories that embarrass or hurt people deeply years after the fact. Many of these stories were told by their siblings with full parental approval. Mike talked about how his brother learned early that he could always elicit a laugh from their taciturn father by recounting the latest pranks the playground bullies had pulled on Mike, who could throw neither a ball nor a punch, unlike the other males in the family. Lorraine recalled that her parents always pitted her and her sister against one another. Whoever was currently in favor got center stage and quickly learned to keep it, at least for a while, by telling tales about the other. "I think that when parents allow kids to tell hurtful stories about each other, it's a kind of thievery," one woman said sadly. "That's what happened in my childhood home, and today I have three sisters I barely know. My heart aches for what we might have been to one another."

Children model the storytelling behavior of their parents, often to the point where they use identical gestures and inflections. Sacred storytelling calls on adult family members to model responsible storytelling and to actively teach children how to tell affirming, redeeming stories that strengthen their relationships. This can be very effective when older siblings are encouraged to honestly and *kindly* tell stories of their own experiences and emotions to help younger ones deal with frightening or confusing situations. Since kids very often look up to their older brothers and sisters, sibling stories can often prove to be more effective than parental ones.

From the time she was very small, my now-thirteen-year-old neighbor, Becky, has entertained me with sweet, funny stories about her older sisters' experiences with school, sports, boys or whatever the issue of the moment happened to be. What I found most delightful was a custom that she and her oldest sister, Cindy (now a graduate student in Boston), developed after Cindy got her driver's license back when she was in high school. Every few months when Cindy is home from college, they make sure to have a girls' night out together. They may hit the mall, take in a movie or go out for ice cream or dinner, but the activity is always less important than the girl talk. It is a way of breaking away from the bustle of a big family and making a lasting connection that bridges both the distance and the ten-year age gap.

Carving out special time between parent and child can likewise encourage children to learn to tell stories. In her delightful audiotape *The Spiritual Power of Storytelling,* Jose Hobday recalls that as a child she always loved Tuesday "because that's the day I met my mother in her girlhood." While working together over the ironing board, Jose and her mom told stories and connected on everything from popular songs to sex education.[3]

When children know they are being listened to, they love to tell stories and take special care to tell them well. But sadly, many no longer make the attempt because they know that Mom's got one eye on the steaks in the broiler, her mind on a new client and her ear cocked for the sound of her pager. Dad rushes in from work, gulps down dinner and races back out to coach soccer. Sometimes parents may seem to be listening, or they may even *try* to listen, but their kids know that the "real world" with all its demands invariably rushes in like white water, swirling them away from the "trivialities" of childhood. So they turn their attention to MTV instead.

Kids who do not get the opportunity to tell their stories with the assurance of being heard are the ones who interrupt adult conversation. They nag, they whine, they tug on the phone cord and insinuate themselves into adult discussions until their parents either give them the spotlight or banish them from the scene. They also grow up to be dismal failures in the art of communication. If you have never been listened to, how can you begin to listen to others? When you have never been a welcome participant in a conversation, how do you know when it is appropriate to talk? When nothing you say is ever important, how can you help but either stop trying or learn to monopolize every discussion in hopes that if you spill enough words a few of them might actually mean something? And how on earth, when you rarely get the chance to test the waters, are you supposed to figure out what interests other people and makes them laugh?

Storytelling civilizes the wildebeest within. Every time your child tells a story, a window of opportunity opens to teach him graciousness. By not embarrassing him and not allowing others to humiliate him for his naive attempts at verbalizing his experiences, you quietly show him what it means to have empathy. By giving him your full attention, you teach him to value what others have to say. By respecting his viewpoint, you teach him tolerance. By taking delight in his wonder, you teach him to wonder about greater things. And by including him in family storytelling, you teach him to love and to be loved.

"But who's got the time?" asked one harried woman. "I hold down a full-time job, have a husband, three kids and a four-bedroom house to take of. I also chair two committees and have to entertain my husband's clients once a month. Time's rushing by like an express train."

That is precisely the point. And when it is gone, it will never, ever come again. It was only yesterday that I stood at O'Hare Airport waiting for a tiny ten-pound baby with peach-fuzz hair and a toothless grin to be carried off the plane. Soon I will be waiting for a lovely, slim young woman who is as tall as I am to walk off the stage carrying a college diploma. You only get one chance to stop by the troll bridge. Don't miss it. Even if the trolls are not around, the lady in the glass house is well worth the trip.

Things to Talk About

1. How has fantasy played a role in your childhood? In the lives of your children? How comfortable are you with it? Why?

2. What memories do you want to make certain your children never forget? What can you do to ensure that they do not?

3. Do your family stories have a civilizing effect on your kids? What about the stories told in your childhood home? Is there a correlation between the two? What can you do to make sure your children are

heard and their stories are valued?

Things to Do

1. Adapt a children's story to the real events in the life of a child you love. Use repetition and invite him to conarrate the tale. Be creative. Add lines of a song, gestures, dance steps or anything else that adds to the fun.

2. Plan to spend special time with each child alone. Tell him stories of your childhood and encourage him to tell you stories too. Ask for details to get a reluctant storyteller interested and be sure he knows he has your undivided attention. Good springboards for stories include hikes, movies, picnics, cooking or any other shared activity you both enjoy. Children's books and old photos can also get stories spinning.

3. Go camping. There is something magical about a campfire. If you are not the outdoors type, "camp out" on the family-room floor on sleeping bags, build a fire in the fireplace, cook hot dogs on a stick over the open flame. Then turn out the lights and let the stories spin.

Seven

Passing
on the Wisdom
The Value of Elder Stories

Iɴ ᴛʜᴇ ʙᴀsᴇᴍᴇɴᴛ, sᴏᴍᴇᴡʜᴇʀᴇ ᴀᴛ ᴛʜᴇ ʙᴏᴛᴛᴏᴍ ᴏꜰ ᴀɴ ᴀɴᴄɪᴇɴᴛ ʙʟᴀɴᴋᴇᴛ chest, there is a stationery box full of those old-fashioned reel-to-reel audiotapes. I have not looked at them in years, but I suspect they have become a tangled wad of magnetic spaghetti by now. Ordinarily I would have tossed them out long ago, except that one of them (if only I knew which) contains the voice of my grandfather, recorded Christmas Day 1964. That was the year I convinced my parents that the only thing standing between me and a brilliant career in journalism was a shiny black Panasonic tape recorder. I barely had it out of the box when my always affable grandfather graciously agreed to become my first interview subject. The most probing question I ever got around to asking him that day was "What did you get for Christmas?" So any chance of our producing a piece of living history or even a compilation of funny stories was pretty much squelched from the get-go.

But if there was one thing my grandfather and I had in common, it was "the gift of gab." We chatted away happily for fifteen minutes,

he in his Irish brogue, me in my giggly "reporter voice," about any
number of zany topics before he topped it off with a spontaneous and
spirited rendition of "It Was Christmas Eve in London." Since he sang
about as well as I interviewed, we lacked a little in technique, but
more than made up for it in charm, wit and enthusiasm. In fact we
put on such a memorable show that to this day my Uncle Jerry, who
lives in Las Vegas, never fails to bring up the infamous "interview"
every time he sees me.

Then came Christmas 1986, and it was déjà vu time. No sooner
had Moira torn the wrapping paper off the tape recorder she had
requested to explore her own possible journalistic talents than she
began scouting the crowd for a possible interview subject. Almost
immediately she hit upon Aunt Peg.

Aunt Peg was not really our aunt. She was Eric's sister's husband's
aunt, but we all called her Aunt Peg anyway, since she seemed to like
it and we liked her. She was in her eighties then and very hard of
hearing, so she did not say too much. But she loved my cooking and
laughed at the kids' antics and always seemed to enjoy our chaotic
Christmases. Getting her to understand that Moira wanted to
interview her was a tricky proposition, but we enunciated exagger-
atedly, pantomimed and engaged the help of her nephew. Eventually
she got the idea. Moira inserted the cassette, pressed the record
button and asked her to talk about growing up alongside the river in
Marietta, Ohio.

When she began, maybe three people were listening. By the time
she wrapped it up two hours later, her star had risen so high and so
bright that it would have blinded the Magi. She talked about big things
like surviving the floods and seeing Haley's Comet, but she also told
us about Christmas trees lit with real candles, her family's building
one of the first duplexes in town, and a mother who made doll clothes.
Then I realized that I'd had the right idea back in 1964 after all. Even
if I had not asked the "right" questions, I *had* managed to preserve
something precious and fleeting as well as give my grandfather a tiny
piece of immortality. Moira had the right idea too—it turned out to
be Aunt Peg's last Christmas.

It used to be (and in some cultures still is) that the younger

members of the tribe would naturally gather at the feet of the elders
to listen to the old stories. It was assumed that if you lived long
enough, you probably knew a thing or two about life. Today if you live
long enough, it is assumed that you will reach obsolescence.

A few months ago, when I was out for a walk, I saw a woman in
late middle age come out of her house to the mailbox. Her hair was
graying and cut in no particular style. She was at least twenty pounds
overweight and was dressed in shapeless brown polyester pants, a
flowered blouse and blue terrycloth house slippers. From out of
nowhere the thought struck me, *She's one of the invisible women.*
The aging process (especially when unkempt and unbridled) is a
spook in society's attic, kept there with poverty, illness and deformity.
As long as we pretend it is not there or refuse to open the attic door,
we can keep our anxiety at bay. But if we sneak so much as a furtive
peek at it, we may experience an urge to run screaming into the night
in mortal terror. Not only are we afraid of facing old age when it visits
somebody else, but we are also afraid of being caught by it ourselves.

For three years I worked in a nursing home as director of
admissions and community relations. What I learned in those
thirty-six months would fill an entire book in itself, but the bottom
line is this: as a society, we are working hard to produce a culture of
perpetual twenty-somethings. If you ever want to be inconspicuous,
all you need to do is put the lid on your jar of alpha-hydroxy anti-aging
cream and let your roots grow out. Get comfortable with yourself and
don't run quite so fast. And if that does not work, just admit you are
aging and you will fade from sight faster than the printed design on a
scrap of cheap cotton cloth.

Don't misunderstand me. I have nothing against trying to stay vital
and active as long as possible. What I want to know is why we cannot
also accept whatever stage of life we are in. I cannot help but wonder
what will happen when the entire adult population is at the same
stage of psychological development, whether they have been on the
planet for twenty-five years or for seventy-five. With everyone moving
and shaking, having babies in their fifties and sixties, and lining up
for liposuction, who will be left to evaluate and summarize our
history, pass on the riches of our culture, point out the error of our

ways and keep the next generation from repeating our mistakes? If a voice cried out in the wilderness, who would ever hear it above the beeping of computers and the blare of rock music?

If we elevated the elderly to the status of sage, as Moses and Abraham are revered in the Bible, the spook might actually depart the attic—or at least not howl quite as loudly. Facing a future of obsolescence and indignity, it is no wonder that we are terrified of growing older. Storytelling is not a magic bullet guaranteed to ricochet us back to our senses, but it is not such a bad a place to start. Maybe if we thought the old stories had value, maybe if we stopped and listened to them, we would learn something, not only about our predecessors but also about ourselves. If old people were valued and listened to, we might actually accept old age with grace and dignity and save ourselves a lot off fruitless and pathetic grief over something that is bound to catch us in the end anyway.

A peculiar thing I have noticed about our world is that experience counts, but only to a point. I remember trying to get my first job. "Come back when you have more experience," they said. And I remember thinking, *But how can I acquire experience if nobody will give me a job?* Eventually I acquired the job and gained the experience, and eventually I moved on to other jobs and other experiences. But all that hard-won experience will count for very little in twenty years, because I will be *old.* I wonder if our zeal for blazing new scientific and technological trails leads us to discount the experiential. How many times have we heard "That's just anecdotal evidence—it doesn't mean a thing," as though any information not garnered through a strict scientific model had less value than an amoeba? Once advancing age tosses you out of the fiber-optic loop, you might as well slink off to your rocking chair in the sunset because your stories, your anecdotal evidence about the meaning of life, are inconsequential.

Hollywood producer and director Garson Kanin tells a delightful story about aging and experience. When a large city experienced a massive blackout, the young engineers in charge of the power plant worked around the clock to get it restored. Finally they had to admit defeat and call in a man in his eighties who had retired from city service some years previously. The old man came in, assessed the situation and asked for a small hammer. With one carefully considered tap he had the darkened city ablaze with light. "That's terrific!" the young engineers enthused. "How much do we owe you?"

"One thousand dollars and two cents," the old man responded.

"One thousand dollars and two cents! But that's ridiculous! All you did was give it one tap with the hammer."

At that the old man just smiled and said, "You're right. The two cents is for the tap and the thousand dollars is for knowing where to make it!"[1]

When we discount the experiential, we cheat the elderly out of their right to a life review. But we cheat ourselves as well. When we forget to ask for the stories or fail to listen to them when they are offered, we set ourselves up for a lifetime of unanswered questions. Once the elders have passed on, it is too late to write down the recipe for Irish soda bread or find out the story behind the heavy crystal bowl that always stood on the deep windowsill in the dining room. Like the words on our computer screens that we carelessly forget to save, pieces of our history are lost forever unless we make an effort to commit them to memory. We also cheat ourselves in another way. If we fail to ask the elders to show us how they accomplished even the most practical things, such as making fruitcake or building a fence, we lose not only the old skills but also the fabric of the culture that produced them.

In 1966 a high-school English teacher named Eliot Wigginton launched a project in Rabun Gap, Georgia, that dramatically underscored the power and value of listening to elder stories, especially those of the common people. Students armed with notebooks and tape recorders were set loose in the Appalachian Mountains to talk with old timers about everything from mountain music and lore to making soap and tanning hides. The Foxfire project, as it came to be known, sparked the imagination of the nation as readers from small hamlets to big cities realized that Foxfire embraced far more than a collection of "quaint" customs, stories and people. As the elders told their stories and shared their skills, they passed on a vibrant culture, a unique worldview and a philosophy of life that had served them for generations. Most importantly, *it still had relevancy*. What began as a school project about mountain customs ultimately spawned the *Foxfire* magazine, ten Foxfire books, a Broadway play and in 1982 the *Foxfire* movie, starring the late Jessica Tandy. The extraordinary legacy of Foxfire is not that it proved to be a commercial success, but that it continues to teach as much about life as it does about playing the dulcimer.[2]

As you begin to encourage your own elderly family members to tell their stories, do not be surprised if you meet with reluctance. Over and over in the nursing home my requests for a story would elicit only, "Oh, you don't want to hear about that" or "I don't have anything interesting to tell. I lived a pretty ordinary life." Though they may not know what captures the attention of the armies of denim-clad men, women and children who speed on past them to the next technological marvel, the elderly suspect (usually rightly) that it is definitely not life on the farm or living with rationing during World War II. Encountering somebody who takes the time to listen often disconcerts older storytellers, and they must be questioned and cajoled for details. But once they feel their audience resting in the palms of their hands, their stories keep getting better and better.[3]

As Aunt Peg sat in our family room that Christmas Day and took us back to the early days of the twentieth century, she became animated and funny—a person we had never met before. I saw the same thing happen three years later in the nursing home, even among the most confused residents. Since short-term memory is more apt to be impaired than long-term, it is quite possible for people in the earlier stages of senility to tell warm, wonderful, accurate stories about their pasts. When I became aware of this, I started a Saturday-morning storytelling group at the nursing home. I had no experience working with the elderly prior to taking that job, but I could not shake the feeling that this was something I could do to help them take back a measure of dignity.

Saturday Stories

About the time that I got the idea for the storytelling group, the nursing home administrator enrolled me in an eight-week crash course in geriatrics. The instructor of the course loved the storytelling idea and suggested I use it for my class project, so there was no way to wriggle out of it, even though last-minute doubts nagged like overdue bills. My simple goals were complex enough to require a miracle. I hoped to rekindle a spark of interest in those who had withdrawn from life and use stories of the past to help ground the more confused storytellers in the present. At the instructor's suggestion, I handpicked six women to invite—three were apathetic and disinterested in their surroundings, and three were "pleasantly confused," which in nursing home parlance means that they could not find their rooms or remember what they ate for lunch (or *if* they ate lunch), but otherwise functioned fairly well and could accurately answer questions about the past.

Unleashing the stories would not be easy, and I knew it. The apathetic women would no doubt sit like stones or complain of boredom, and the confused would either wander off the subject or just wander off. I had to find something to engage their interest and especially their senses. My hunch was that sensory stimulation triggers memories faster and with more immediacy than questions or even stories. Who hasn't felt a warm summer breeze and been transported back to another time? Or caught a whiff of baking apples and felt a stab of longing for the pies Grandma used to make back in the apartment on 57th Street? I decided to select a different theme each week and bombard them with as many sensory experiences as possible.

Vivaldi's *The Four Seasons* played softly in the background that first rainy Saturday morning as I nervously arranged a gigantic vase of dripping yellow daffodils picked from my backyard less than an hour before. Next to it I laid out the rest of my props—a bag of fresh potting soil, a trowel, an assortment of flower seed packets and a stack of clay pots. All around the room bright yellow posterboard splashed with pictures of lavish flower gardens and blow-ups of spectacular individual specimens added a riot of color to the concrete-block walls of the activities room. All six invitees showed up, but, as I had expected, three of them were not happy about it. "What's this junk for? I'm missing the Indians game," Alina grumbled as she wheeled herself into the room.

"They're having that vegetable soup for lunch today," Carol complained, lighting up a cigarette. "I hate the stuff. And I'm not helping you plant any flowers either, I'll tell you that right now."

"That long-haired music gets on my nerves," Ella informed me flatly.

Two of the confused residents, Sadie and Bertha, on the other hand, were enchanted. They sniffed the flowers, waltzed with each other to the music and told me everything was "just beautiful, honey." Unfortunately, their enthusiasm served only to irritate the three complainers. LaVerne, who looked like a dreamy, remote Katharine Hepburn, as usual said nothing. To top it off, Hazel, a woman with advanced Alzheimer's, wandered into the room and began "straightening" things and humming to herself. It was so dismal a beginning that even Norman Vincent Peale would have had to struggle to find a bright side. But I had committed myself to at least six weeks of storytelling, so there was nothing to do but get through it.

I began by asking them to remember what it felt like to go outside in the early morning when the dew lay sparkling on the grass like scattered rhinestones, to listen to the silence of the early morning, broken only by the songs of the birds. We took a moment to close our eyes and let the music wash over us. Then we smelled the dirt, planted the seeds and talked about all the aspects of flower gardens, from the work they involved to the pleasure they gave the spirit. I told a little story about how my grandfather always picked peonies on Memorial Day to take to the cemetery to decorate his sister's grave and how once someone had dug up the peony bush the night before Memorial Day and stolen it away.

At that Carol let out a sharp, barking laugh and told us how she used to run out the back door with a broom and chase the neighborhood kids out of her own garden. Then she told the story of how she made all the floral arrangements for her daughter's wedding. Sadie told about how she sometimes pinned a flower to her dress when she sold magazines at the bus station, and Ella said that she had once kept house "for the rich people" with an Italian gardener who floated flowers in the swimming pool.

"Did you know that some flowers are edible?" LaVerne asked

suddenly. "I used to candy violets to decorate my daughter's birthday cake." Surprisingly, Ella, who prided herself on being a great cook and had no patience with confused residents, found this a fascinating piece of trivia. For about five seconds I credited myself with having pulled off a major coup as I watched her listen carefully while a "pleasantly confused" woman told her step by step how it is done. But then I looked over at Alina and saw the tears rolling like rain down the grooves of her face.

"Alina, what's wrong?" I asked, my heart starting to pound.

For several excruciating seconds the tears continued to flow silently. "It reminds me of my garden in Colorado Springs," she whispered finally. "It makes me want to go home."

"Flowers make me sad too," LaVerne added, "because you know the beauty can't last forever."

Panic! The conversation had taken a sudden, unexpected melancholy turn, and I did not have the foggiest notion how to bring it back to "safe" ground. To interrupt with some cheery little story seemed phony, but the thought of ending with everyone depressed produced so much anxiety I would have done almost anything to garner a laugh. I decided to ride it out and see if the talk swung back to a cheerier theme naturally.

It didn't.

We wound up the session with Alina telling the story of how she had never wanted to come back to Ohio in the first place, but had done so at her daughter's insistence. She said that every morning the first thing she thought of was the sight of mountains out her kitchen window and how warm the stone path in her backyard used to feel under her bare feet. As I took the flower posters off the wall, I felt like a miserable failure.

My instructor was elated. "Don't you see what happened?" she asked. "You made them *feel*." *Yes, feel miserable*, I thought. Even as I was planning it, I was already dreading next Saturday's session.

Over the weeks that followed we talked about baking, weddings, old toys, cars, going to school, cleaning house and county fairs. Pretty safe stuff, right? Wrong. Those six women lifted me to the heights of heaven and cast me to the depths of hell with their stories. You name the emotion and we encountered it, put it out on the table and talked about it. We dealt with laughter, love, anger, embarrassment, guilt, resentment, sorrow and regret. By the time the eight weeks were over, every idealistic notion I ever had about running a nice little storytelling group lay shattered in a million shards. I had wanted a safe stroll down memory lane and wound up with a group of people wrestling with the memories of a lifetime and trying to make of them something whole and cohesive.

What I learned from that experience was this: nobody needed me to orchestrate their feelings or make everything "okay." My job was not to whitewash real feelings of guilt and regret, but to listen as they went about the *necessarily* difficult business of trying to extract wisdom and meaning from the pain of the past. To pat them on the head and say "It's okay; it doesn't matter" would have been both patronizing and demeaning. Those women were embarking on one of the most important missions of human life—conducting a life review in preparation for dying. My squeamishness at the first sign of painful emotions was nothing more than my own fear of old age masquerading as concern. I did not want to face the fact that they knew the limitations of their life span, and I especially did not want to think that someday I too might look back at my life with that much longing, regret, anger and sadness. But in our misguided attempt to "protect" the elderly from negative emotions, we only continue the pillaging of their dignity.

"This is the best part of the week," LaVerne said on our third Saturday.

"Why do you say that?" I asked.

"Because the stories play in my head over and over like movies all the time. Until now there's been nobody but me to watch them."

It took many more Saturdays to realize that I received the miracle I hoped for; in fact, I had had it all along, from that very first morning. The miracle, of course, was Alina's tears, which in time taught us how to be real with one another.

A Matter of Dignity
Being real, uncovering a bit of soul, is what family storytelling is all

about. Entertainment is a byproduct—a good one of course—but still a byproduct. When you allow your elderly family members to feel their feelings and tell their stories, you give them back the humanity that our youth culture snatches away. Nothing brings anyone alive faster than genuine interest. Just an hour ago I was "zonking out" at the computer screen, glancing at the clock more often than I should, each finger as heavy as a ten-pound weight. Suddenly the telephone at my right elbow shrilled and I snapped awake to learn that Moira's college roommate, Betsy, needed to interview a writer for her journalism class. Suddenly I was bright, animated, talking a mile a minute, as alert as if I had just returned from an adventure. Human beings, whether they are eight or eighty, blossom like hot-house orchids when asked to share the things that matter to them.

Julia, a nurse, told me that last summer she was seriously worried about her mother. After her husband died, she sold her big colonial house and moved into a small condo. Though the move was voluntary, it seemed to have thrown her into a depression. "She kept saying, 'I might as well die. Nobody needs an old baggage like me around,' " Julia recalls. "To be honest, I was getting tired of hearing it. I had enough problems of my own without listening to her whine."

Then in May a young couple moved into the unit next door. The wife, a teacher, was home during the summer, and she soon developed the habit of stopping by late in the afternoon for iced tea and conversation. Before long, Julia's mother was sharing recipes, showing her how to get coffee stains out of a tablecloth, explaining which plants acted as natural pesticides in the garden and counseling her about marriage.

"It was wonderful," Julia said. "The more she shared her stories and knowledge, the more vital she even *looked.* And to think we had almost let this vitality slip through our fingers! I was even a little jealous, if you want to know the truth. I got to thinking, *Is there more to this mother I love, but who makes me crazy, than meets the eye?*"

There was. And uncovering it was discovering pentimento. Like oil paint on an aging canvas, the passion that lay beneath the overlay of her mother's conventional life became transparent. Suddenly complaints seemed more like longings, despair more like a desire for encouragement. And best of all, the more they talked, the more clearly hints of a long-buried sense of possibility began to shine through the loneliness. As Julia began to connect with her mother on a level beyond the everyday patter about health, safety, food and finances, she met a woman she never dreamed existed. "My mother had wanted to be an artist," she says with wonderment. "It was the first I'd ever heard of it. I mean she was always good at decorating and flower arranging, but the only paintbrush I'd ever seen her wield was the one she used to paint the kitchen."

Wisely, Julia outfitted her mother with art supplies and encouraged her to paint. "She's painting her stories," she says, pulling out an unframed canvas covered with a striking, almost luminescent watercolor of a seascape. "This is Lake George in the Adirondacks, where she spent her childhood summers. She painted it from memory. And there's the little boat she and her sister learned to sail. It's like through her painting she's connecting with her stories and through her stories she's connecting with us. I feel as though she's taking us back with her on a journey through her life."

The journey back is every bit as essential as the journey forward. By telling the stories of who they once were, what they dreamed of, what they accomplished and what they failed to do, the elderly reclaim the parts of themselves lost through disease, infirmity and isolation. Even when they can no longer care for themselves or participate actively in family life, it is the stories that will salvage their self-worth.

Mike found this out last year when his father, Harold, suffered a major stroke and had to be placed in a nursing home. He lost the ability to walk, form words and even take care of his most basic needs. He spent most of his final days lying curled up in a hospital bed or slumped in a wheelchair. "The staff took care of him, and for the most part, did an okay job," Mike says. "But they treated him like a child. Oh man, I gotta tell you, it was the toughest thing I ever did to go in there and watch some twenty-year old twit say to this man who'd been president of a bank, 'Hey you! Stop that yelling! You'll get your dinner when you behave yourself.' " He looks away and takes a deep breath before continuing. "I know they were overworked and understaffed, but my father was nothing more than a noisy *body* to them."

Change came only when one of the aides, an older woman who had worked in nursing homes all her life, suggested that he bring in some photos of his father taken at various stages of his life from the time he was a child to the previous year when he had stood on the deck of a cruise ship bound for Alaska with his wife and two friends. Mike took her advice, and before long other family members brought in additional things—the duck decoy their father had carved, a pennant from the Kiwanis Club he had belonged to and pictures of his grandchildren. When an aide or a nurse came in to turn him in the bed or administer a medication, a visiting family member would tell the caretaker a story, perhaps about how Harold fought in World War II and had to leave behind a wife who realized she was pregnant the week after his departure. They talked about the Christmases when he played Santa Claus at the party for the bank employees' children and how at every Sunday dinner he pulled the wishbone of the chicken with a different child, who always got the longest side.

"What happened wasn't perfect, but it was a big improvement," Mike recalls. "One time my mom went in to visit and she heard an aide talking to him about the wishbones, about how she did that with her own kids. By then he was barely conscious, so I don't know whether or not he heard. But at least he'd become a *person* again. That's what mattered to me most."

Easier Access

Each time dignity is bestowed, it gifts the bestower as well as the recipient. By listening to the stories of the elderly with interest and respect and by telling their stories when they can no longer tell them for themselves, we acknowledge the dignity of the human experience universal to us all. We acknowledge, too, our sense of connection and remind ourselves to value, tell and seek meaning from the stories of our own lives. But the time for listening is fleeting. If we are not willing to gather at the feet of the elders *right now* in the midst of the most hectic decades of our lives, it is unreasonable to assume that anyone will pause in the coming chaos to gather and listen to our stories when we become the elders.

If you are like many people I have talked with, you may be feeling a little uncomfortable at this point. More than any other aspect of storytelling, elder stories created the most discomfort during my interviews—and not just because the elderly stand as reminders that our life on earth is finite. While many people expressed a belief in the necessity of elder stories and desired to make time for them, they also admitted to finding it difficult, if not altogether impossible, to listen to their parents' stories. "To listen to the stories in which I played a role is torture," one bright, articulate woman offered, "because while my parents are busy painting a pretty picture of the past, I'm flooded with all the attendant feelings that were anything but pleasant for me."

"Even after all these years there's still a hidden agenda," a forty-five-year-old man, a successful accountant, said flatly. "Everything still points up the thousand and one ways I let them down."

"I hate when my mother tells stories because everything is so exaggerated. If I won the spelling bee in a sixth-grade class of twelve kids, she tells it like there were six hundred competitors. It's like nothing is ever good enough as it really was. In bragging me up, she makes me feel worthless as I really am."

"My father is a manipulator. Always was, always will be. He jerks around the facts to make himself look good. He refuses to acknowledge his own actions and the damage it did to all of us. Maybe I could forgive him if he stopped rationalizing."

Ideally elderhood is a time for reflection and spiritual growth, as well as a time for forgiveness and the healing of past pain. But not everyone experiences this ideal, and some die exactly as they lived. Nowhere is that more evident than in the nursing home. During the three years I worked there I saw many, many people die. Some of them left this world emotionally, if not physically, estranged from their children, complaining, playing mind games and causing problems right up until the moment they drew their very last breath. Advanced age, I was quick to discover, does not automatically confer wisdom. Yet I also learned that very often the people who cause the most distress are the ones who wrestle with the biggest demons. In the end, each of us is responsible for our own life review. You cannot force anyone to see the stories as you see them, nor can you push them toward a level of spiritual development that they are clearly not ready for. All you can do is offer them the gift of compassion.

In the letter to the Hebrews the Bible says, "He can deal gently with the ignorant and wayward, since he himself is beset with weakness" (Heb 5:2). We all have our share of irrationality, stubbornness and denial. When we acknowledge our own failures, we take the first step toward compassion because we shift the emphasis off our own egos *no matter how justified we may be in harboring our hurts* and admit to being broken in places too. This does not mean that you have to silently accept stories you find painful. It is okay, and possibly healing, to say, "That's not the way I remember that, Mom. To me, it was . . ." as long as your objective is not to retaliate for past wrongs or to extract an omission of guilt at any price. Compassion calls us to set aside both the need to be right and the need to control, and to accept the fact that sometimes the only thing that can be changed is our attitude.

If your relationship with your parents has been painful, it is not wise to begin a life review with the stories in which you play a role. Instead, lead the storyteller back to the beginning of his life. Urge him to tell you about his childhood, his parents, what it felt like to grow up in his home. Ask him about his friends, what gave him joy, when he first fell in love, how he met your mother, how he chose his life's work and what it meant to him. By encouraging him to tell the stories in which you are conspicuously absent you distance yourself enough to listen with less judgment and less emotion. As you gain insight into the forces that shaped him, it may become easier to understand the behaviors that caused you pain and, ultimately, to find healing.

But sometimes it is simply not possible to distance yourself from the past firmly enough to engage in life-review storytelling with an aged parent beyond the most superficial level. Adult children who still bleed and chafe sometimes lack the emotional strength to confront agonizing issues, especially when they have struggled a lifetime to find and maintain a superficial peace with a parent who clings to his own justifications. An unexpected encounter with the daughter of one of my favorite nursing home residents showed me that we must prayerfully decide what we are capable of doing in any given relationship.

One evening I was working late when Paulina, a woman in her early fifties and a devout Roman Catholic, stopped by my office, clearly distraught. She sank down in the chair in front of my desk and began to weep. When she could finally speak, anger licked at her words like flames. "Everybody around here thinks my mother is so cute," she cried, "but they don't have to be her daughter! She's always so nice to them, and she cries and tells them how I don't care about her, and now to them, I'm the Bad Daughter. What they don't see is that I'm doing the best I can. She's so demanding and critical that it takes everything I have to show up here, and then the staff acts like I'm cold and heartless. They expect me to do what can only be done if you've had a close, loving relationship with your mother—which I most certainly haven't!"

As her story poured out, I found that I was not surprised to learn that the charming, gracious lady I knew and the terror Paulina described were the same person. Somehow I had always known that Maria's children labored to "do the right thing" by her. My admiration for the woman in front of me was boundless and so was my sympathy. She was indeed doing her best, and the price she was paying for it was evident in her haggard face and sagging shoulders. "Paulina," I said finally, "you *are* doing your best. I know it and you know it. Maybe the best way to take care of your mother right now is to keep doing what you can and let us do what you can't."

She looked relieved, as though someone had removed a heavy burden from her shoulders. "Are you saying that if I encourage her relationship with you and the others around here, I am not abandoning her, but maybe helping her?"

"I am. It's an act of love to make sure she gets what she needs. As for the staff, it doesn't matter what they think, because you know in your heart that you want the best for your mother and you're making sure she gets it."

After that, I began to spend more and more time talking with Maria.

Because we did not share a lifetime of emotional baggage, I could listen to her stories without judgment. I could laugh, cry, commiserate—do whatever was required from the vantage point of distance. Maria was afraid to die, afraid even to be in a nursing home, and she realized early on that the best defense was to make sure she was surrounded by people who loved her, which I did, even though I harbored no illusions about the kind of parent she had been. Over time we talked about many things, but never once did she admit that she had been anything less than a long-suffering mother who gave her "ungrateful" children everything she had and more. I came to the conclusion that just because what Maria gave them was not nearly enough does not mean it was not real. She did the best she could, given her own past, her emotional makeup and her limited understanding of children. She could not imagine that anything had been lacking.

As for Paulina, she visited once a week, did her mother's shopping, painted her long, beautifully manicured nails, brought her homemade gristoli, the thin, crisp Italian cookies that made her dark eyes sparkle with delight, and encouraged her to talk about her girlhood in Italy. They listened to Puccini's operas together, Paulina wrote down the family recipes, and they made a tape recording of her mother talking about "the old country." It was not perfect, certainly, but it was better by far than breaking open old wounds and wrangling over events that would never be resolved.

Dealing with a painful history can cast a shadow over a process that should be as natural as breathing. But as Paulina slowly discovered, there are ways to honor the elder and conserve important stories that shed light on your family's history without causing undue pain. One of them is to allow someone who is either closer to the storyteller or shares less history with him to facilitate the storytelling process. It is especially fitting and meaningful to allow a grandchild to assume the role of questioner, as I questioned my grandfather in 1964. When an elder looks behind him, what does he see but children moving forward to someday take his place? And what do the children see in front of them but the long line of ancestors who paved their way? To engage grandparent and grandchild in a process as old as human history is to symbolically acknowledge the truth that the past and future converge at the place where the stories begin.

Another way to give yourself some breathing space is to approach storytelling in a more formal, ritualistic manner. Gather the entire family for dinner and an evening of taped storytelling, perhaps spread out over several sessions. Have the "story prompts" prepared in advance and let the grandchildren take turns asking the questions. You can either correlate the taping with an important occasion, such as a birthday or an anniversary, or make the event an occasion in itself. Either way, you are surrounding the storyteller with love and attention and making her feel special, while at the same time providing an element of safety for those whose emotions are too raw to listen in a more intimate setting.

Creating New Stories

It is essential to remember that because life is always creative, elder stories are not solely about history. Overemphasizing the past can lead us to forget that the elderly continue to amass new experiences and emotions every day and often continue to learn, discover and make plans for the future. For Julia, the nurse whose mother acted on a long-buried passion to paint, the immediate moment provided a much less stressful entry point to the stories than the past. Once the desire to create art had been rekindled, life rushed in stronger and more vibrant than ever before. Julia slipped in and joined her mother in its flow.

Oscar Wilde once said, "The muddle of old age is not that one is old, but that one is young." Many elderly people continue to create new stories right up to the end of their lives, despite a society that stubbornly refuses to understand that wrinkles and arthritis can mask a spirit that soars with zest and curiosity. Georgia O'Keefe painted into her nineties, Armand Hammer built the Occidental Petroleum Company in his eighties, Grandma Moses began an art career at seventy-two, Colonel Harlan Sanders launched the Kentucky Fried Chicken restaurants with part of his first social security check, and one of my favorite authors, May Sarton, published the last of her successful journals at eighty-two. As long as there is life, opportunities for story making abound.

An activities director who works with the "well elderly" in a neighborhood community center told me an amusing story that illustrates just how true this is. Several years ago, before home computers were as common as TVs, Carolyn arranged a field trip to take the center's "regulars" to the local vocational school for a hands-on experience in the computer lab. Twenty people signed up for the trip, though some were openly dubious about what could be gained from it and were far more interested in the lunch to follow. The plan was to pair each participant with a student who would personally guide them on their maiden voyage into cyber space.

One querulous participant was Sara, who at eighty-something had very definite opinions about everything. When she saw that she had been paired with a boy who sported an earring and wore his orange hair sculpted like a bowl of stiff meringue, she clamped her lips in a forbidding frown and sat down at the screen with her arms folded across her chest. Her would-be teacher was no doubt equally wary, but he bravely booted up the computer and began to introduce her to DOS and RAM. Slowly Sara's arms uncrossed. She leaned forward and began to tentatively tap a few keys. Suddenly her eyes lit up. "Why, this reminds me of when I used to work!" she exclaimed. "I was one of the first people to be trained on the early IBM keypunch machines."

"Hey, cool," the earringed boy said. "You wanna play some games? I got Jeopardy!" Like most of the center's regulars, Sara never missed a single evening of the popular TV game show and prided herself on answering no fewer than twenty questions correctly each time. Two hours later she and her computer buddy were having so much fun competing that they had to be pried loose from the machine. Later that evening she entertained her family with a funny account of how she had mastered the bits and the bytes with the help of a "darling young man with an earring."

The other evening, just at sunset, I stepped out of the grocery store into a light so surreal that for a nanosecond I thought the world was ending. The sun had broken through a patch of gunmetal sky and was bathing the hillside in a radiant light, the quality of which I had never seen before. Even the air had a hushed, suspended feeling, as though waiting for an apparition. For several minutes I stood in the parking lot, totally transfixed, overcome with a ridiculous, giddy joy, and watched as an enormous technicolor rainbow formed a perfect arch over the highway.

Elder stories remind me of that rainbow in many ways. They explore the full spectrum of life's colors and curve across the span of time, bridging the gap between youthful desire and seasoned wisdom. But most of all, like the rainbow, they offer the promise of a pot of gold. You can find it right at the point where the earth meets the sky.

Things to Talk About

1. How do you think our society moved toward becoming a youth culture? Why do you think it happened?

2. What are the ramifications of everybody looking twenty-five? What do you think will happen when the baby boomers reach elderhood? Will our stories be valued?

Things to Do Right Now

1. Plan to make an audio- or videotape of an elderly family member. Make it a special event. Send out invitations and work together to draw up a list of questions or topics to be covered. Be sure the storyteller feels special and understands why you value what he has to say.

2. Ask one of your family's elders to share her skill or specialized knowledge with you. It could be anything—cooking, whittling, tatting, home remedies or pruning a tree. Pay attention to what it teaches you about life.

3. Make it a point to ask the elders to tell you the story behind the familiar objects in their homes. They do not have to be certifiable antiques, or even costly or unique. Sometimes the best stories arise from such utilitarian items as the cream pitcher that has had a broken handle for twenty years or the dime-store frog figurine.

Eight

Unraveling the Yarns
Claiming the Storytelling Tradition

F OR THE PAST SEVERAL WEEKS A SMALL, QUIET MIRACLE HAS BEEN TAK-
ing place on our side porch. A mother robin built her nest on top of
an enormous straw wreath and laid her eggs. Though her timing was
off (we had planned to screen in the porch at the first sign of spring),
we soon decided that the delay was insignificant in light of having
been chosen for such an honor. We named her Catherine after the
main character in Karen Cushman's Newbery Honor novel,
Catherine, Called Birdy.[1] "Hi, Catherine," we say whenever we walk
by. Her only reply is to fix us with an intense, black-eyed stare.

Last week we began to notice that she was gone for longer periods
of time, so we got a ladder from the garage and climbed up to take a
careful peek inside the nest. Three fuzzy babies immediately raised
their heads, stretched their long necks and opened beaks the color
of pumpkin in hopes of receiving a fat, juicy worm. Suburban dwellers
that we are, we do not often get to experience nature so intimately,
so of course we fell madly, deeply, hopelessly in love.

Not long after that, I was out for a walk when I chanced on a scene so delightful that I stood stock-still on the sidewalk and stared, wondering even then why in the world I was so smitten by the sight of four battered Samsonite suitcases (the hard kind you rarely see anymore) lined up along a curved path leading to the front door of an elegant brick house. Three of them were closed, but the blue cosmetic case closest to the door lay open and empty. It was midday, a brilliant sun burned overhead, and there wasn't a soul in sight. I laughed right out loud at the ridiculous poetry of it.

Every day, life offers up small treasures that produce awe, inspiration and laughter. But often they are either unnoticed or quickly forgotten, shared with no one. Sometimes we even say to ourselves, "I want to remember this." But two seconds later we have become so intent on the need to fertilize the begonias and stop at the store for hairspray on the way home from work that we promptly forget.

To keep ourselves from being robbed of the small graces that provide us with endless stories, it is essential that we firmly turn our backs on the socially ingrained need for perfection, which is largely unattainable and not even worth the effort. Striving to have a "perfect" house, a "perfect" job and "perfect" children impedes story making and squeezes the juice out of our lives. Elisabeth Kübler-Ross, who pioneered the field of death and dying research, said in an article in the *National Catholic Reporter* that when people are in the process of dying what they remember most are the moments spent in communion with other human beings, laughing, having fun, listening, sharing, watching breathtaking sunsets and sitting around campfires.

"It's a silent, meaningful companionship that has meaning and that lasts for decades," she said. "Those are the moments dying patients remember and with smiles on their faces."[2] At the time of death, living at the "right" address, driving the "right" car and keeping the cleanest, most well-organized household in the neighborhood are insignificant. Neither does anyone leave this world wondering whether the heat ducts have been vacuumed. The biblical story of Martha and Mary speaks eloquently to this problem of perpetual busyness. When Jesus came to visit the two sisters in their home, Mary at once sank to the floor at his feet to soak up his stories, while

Martha fussed about the kitchen being the "perfect" hostess. Finally Martha complained to Jesus that she was the one doing all the work and tried to persuade him to tell Mary to get up and help her. To this, Jesus replied, "Martha, Martha, you are anxious and troubled about many things; one thing is needful. Mary has chosen the good portion" (Lk 10:41-42).

Choose the good portion! Celebrate and remember the fruits of the universe! Over the years, I have tried to learn what it takes to capture the precious moments of life. First, you have to really be there in the moment. Look closely. Listen hard. Touch, smell and taste whenever possible. Then go over the experience in fine detail and imprint it on your mind. In her audiotape *The Spiritual Power of Storytelling,* Jose Hobday says that when she was growing up in the Mesa Verde area of the Southwest, her mother urged her to remember the sight of the sleeping Ute, a magnificent mountain configuration resembling an Indian in full war bonnet lying in repose. In the evening, just at sunset when the sky becomes a watercolor and the quality of light is at its tenderest, she would urge her small daughter to come outside and "memorize the land" so that if she grew up and moved far away, she could assuage her loneliness for her childhood home by bringing back a memory so pure and so vivid that it reverberated in every fiber of her being. "Some day you'll find that your heart is yearning to see this again," she wisely counseled. "And you don't want it to be just a sketch. You want it to be clear in colors, you want to know where the lines are, you want to take this to heart."

We do not "take to heart" much of what we see, unfortunately, because we are mentally dashing to the next thing while still in the throes of the last. Just the other day I went out to buy a new faucet set for the bathtub and bought one with only two knobs when I needed three. I spend *hours* in that tub, but I had no idea what kind of plumbing it required. This may be a trivial matter, but it is an unwelcome reminder that despite my efforts to the contrary, I still tend to zip through life only half aware of my surroundings. Becoming more mindful of each precious moment and detail of life is a prerequisite to telling stories that sing and dance with life, because it is the details that create the magic, and it is the details that will make the magic last when the story is over.

Saint Hildegard of Bingen, the Benedictine nun whose music has recently become fashionable again, wrote these words during the tenth century: "Humans grasp and know everything in creation with their five senses. They love with their faces, taste with their lips, analyze by hearing, seek with the scent that pleases them, and act with the feeling that makes them happy. And in doing this they have God, the Creator of everything, as their model."[3]

Once you have taken in every nuance of an experience so that it is etched it in your memory, the third thing you have to do to capture the moment is to tell somebody about it as soon as you can—turn it into story. I cannot promise that you will remember it forever, but I do know that every time you share even the smallest segment of life, your spirit will hold fast to the joy, laughter or awe, even if your conscious mind buries whatever inspired it too deep for easy retrieval. The act of telling the story also gives you the opportunity to relive the experience. Who has not sparkled with the pleasure of sharing the story of hitting the home run that won that game or describing the enormous stag glimpsed through an opening in the woods? That jolt of almost electrical excitement reminds us that we are animated by the Spirit of God.

I hope that by now you are enthusiastic about the benefits and the possibilities of family storytelling and are eager to begin claiming the tradition for your own family. One of the easiest ways to take your place in the long line of storytellers, which stretches back to the beginning of time, is to enter it where you are at this moment. Storytelling is not a complicated art, but we often make it so by thinking that anything less than a four-alarm event is not worthy of being called story. Yet it is our awareness of the small things, which make us human and connects us to life in all its richness, that gives us fodder for most of the stories we tell. If we waited for cosmic events to take place before we told a story, we would exist in a dry and barren landscape, separated from the relentless vitality and energy of the universe. I am reminded of the writings of May Sarton and Gladys Taber, both of whom produced their best autobiographical work as elderly women living alone outside small, rural New England towns.

They filled whole books with simple stories about the weather, nature, pets, gardens, friends, food and work. There was not a murder, a corporate buy-out or a romantic tryst in the lot, yet they mesmerized a vast and varied audience simply by bringing their harried readers back into the thrum of life at its most elemental level and, therefore, back in touch with their authentic selves.

To see storytelling potential in the small dailiness of life, you have to tap into the "sacred now," which means temporarily taking your mind off the report due next Friday and off rising tuition costs, and allowing yourself to be charmed by still-art suitcases and the daily doings of robins. At first it takes concentrated effort, but as you get into the flow, you will find yourself meeting God at every turn. Suddenly when someone asks you what happened today, your answer becomes an enthusiastic "Wait till I tell you!" rather than a flat, sullen "Not much." The word *enthusiasm* actually derives from the Greek words *en* and *theos,* literally, "filled with God."

As you begin to grow in awareness and appreciation of life's small blessings, two transformative things begin to happen. You find yourself infinitely less self-absorbed and more aware of your family and consequently more connected with them. You will even begin to see the world through their eyes and will actively seek out and remember the things that will delight or interest them. One mom mentioned that her eleven-year-old son is so crazy about hot air balloons that they float across the wallpaper border in his bedroom, decorate the covers of his notebooks and work their way into almost every one of his school projects from history to math. One day while she was out doing errands, she sighted several brilliantly colored balloons hovering low in the sky just beyond the local farmer's market. On a whim, she followed them in her car and found herself being invited to bring her son to help tether one the following Sunday. "I went for Joey's sake," she says. "Little did I know that we'd have such an adventure! But what really knocked me out was his face when I told him that his practical old mom had gone chasing after a balloon just for him."

While I have devoted a great deal of attention to stories that families create together, these stories represent only a fraction of the possibilities that await you when you become attuned to family storytelling. Equally important are the personal stories we tell each other of the time spent apart because these are the gateways that spiritually and emotionally connect us again at the end of the day, the business trip or the semester. Whenever you share a personal experience, and especially what that experience meant to you, you invite your family into your private world. At a soul level, each of us already knows what an intimate gift this is, because each time we return home we decide, consciously or unconsciously, how much we will reveal and how much we will withhold of our thoughts, feelings and activities. Even very young children sense this, as evidenced by their often-evasive replies to such questions as "What did you do at school today?" or "How was the party?" Even three- and four-year-olds can be remarkably private at times.

There is a TV commercial that raises my hackles every time I see it. An actor stands next to one of the chrome-and-vinyl kitchen table sets that were popular during the fifties urging families to have dinner together. Every time it comes on, I fight the urge to throw hard objects at the screen. In its attempt to get families to spend more time together, it totally misses the point that what we do around the dinner table is far more significant than the act of sitting there. In too many households the dinner hour is akin to the Grand Inquisition. Barbed words, pointed questions, accusations, lectures, blame and shame get flung across the meatloaf, leaving stomachs twisted into knots and brows furrowed into deep ridges. The dinner hour should be a sacred time set aside for each person to share small stories of the things that brought pleasure or puzzlement that day. It is a delightful, healthful, natural way for families to reconnect and teach their children how to become storytellers.

Digging Deeper

As you begin to make storytelling a part of your daily life, you will soon discover how current events have a way of triggering memories of the past. The other night Caitie was telling us the story (complete with demonstration) of how she had taught our cat, Jazz, to slam-dunk a fuzzy pink ball into Eric's size 12EE shoe on command.

Once we stopped laughing at this uncharacteristic performance (Jazz ordinarily has a definite "cattitude"), we began reminiscing about the many felines that have made their home with us over the past twenty-six years. I told the story of how Leo got his tail cut off in the door. Eric remembered the way Riley used to lie so still in a showcase at our store that customers often mistook him for the handiwork of a taxidermist. Moira told how Suzy Wong used to sleep on top of the refrigerator, draped over the bananas. By the time we wound down, we were astonished to see that half an hour had flown by. To a casual observer it might have seemed an idle amusement, but in that half-hour we affirmed shared history, connected with each other in the present and reminded ourselves of the meaning and the pleasure animals bring to our lives.

Old photos also provide a sure-fire entry point to stories of the past, especially when you are trying to extract remembrances from an elderly family member who may be reluctant or uncertain where to begin. Take down the family album or show slides or videos of family holidays, vacations and special events and watch what happens. Last summer Jeannie and her husband, Garrett, hosted an enormous family reunion that drew people from seven states, England and Bermuda. Since many members of this diverse group had not been together in a decade and others had never met any extended family at all, they were justifiably concerned about how to make everyone feel welcome and, most of all, connected. Jeannie hit on the idea of asking each group to bring a favorite family photo and be prepared to tell a story about either the event or the person it depicted.

"We had everything from old sepia-colored daguerreotypes in those little velvet-lined cases to the crazy pictures amusement parks take when you're riding the roller coaster," she reported. "It might sound weird if you haven't experienced it. But as people shared their stories, I felt this rush of something—I don't even know what to call it—pride, I guess. For weeks afterward I found myself thinking about the stories, especially those about relatives I'd never known. It was so strange to see in them elements of myself."

When I was a child, I used to cajole my father for months to show old home movies. Maybe once a year he would agree, and for days in advance I was in a frenzy of excitement at the chance to meet my younger selves again, especially two-year-old me dancing the hula in a tiny grass skirt. It was a sight that never failed to fill me with almost hysterical delight. Even as I write this, I can still feel the delicious thrill of anticipation as he unfurled the screen, hung it from a clothes hanger on the back of a kitchen chair and unpacked the heavy black projector from its tattered yellow box. "Douse the lights!" he'd call out and then flip a switch to flood the screen with a beam of intense white light.

The projector was inevitably too high or too low, so he had to add or subtract telephone books and old copies of *Reader's Digest* to find the ideal height. My sister and I would seize the moment to dance and cavort and make bunny-ear silhouettes on the screen. It was only when the bright, jerky, flashing lights signaled the start of the reel that we collapsed in a heap on the floor, held our breath and waited for the stories to emerge like living things to join us there in the dark.

Not long ago Caitie happened to spot on a table in my parents' living room a small black-and-white photo none of us could recall ever having seen before of my sister's third birthday. Though the day itself remains elusive, the sight of Colleen and me as small children standing around a homemade birthday cake with our grandparents, who have been dead for more than twenty years, flooded me with memories. A few days later I was sitting on the porch reading and absent-mindedly ran my thumb along the arm of the rocking chair. The smooth, varnished feel of the wood startled me, and I looked down at it in amazement. While my mind was engaged with Madeleine L'Engle's *The Rock That Is Higher,* my fingers were remembering the sensation of piercing the hot, red blisters on the arms of my grandparents' porch chairs. Thirty years later I momentarily expected once again to peel off the rubbery paint in long scarlet ribbons.

Kinesthetic memory, the kind that is stored in our nerve endings, is a stunning phenomenon. If you have not experienced it, try this experiment. Look around your home and randomly select an item from the past that tells a story, perhaps your grandfather's old wood plane that sits unused on a shelf in the family room. Pick it up and glide your fingers over the burled finish. Close your eyes, be still for a moment, and allow it take you back to those long-ago afternoons when you stood at the workbench in his small detached garage next to a scraggly thicket of rosebushes watching him turn wood into satin while the bees hummed in the pink blossoms outside the crooked window. Picture his gnarled, grease-stained hands with their prominent knuckles maneuvering the plane with great skill while your own stubby fingers held on to the edge of the paint-spattered workbench. Listen closely and hear the dusty old radio on the shelf next to the gray metal oil can playing Tommy Dorsey. Feel the hard-packed dirt floor against your bare, sweaty feet and see the motes of dust dancing in the sunlight. Everything you need to take you back, including the smell of the cedar shavings, is there, captured forever in the feel of the plane in your hand.

Stories are conjured like ghosts from the mists of memory. To call them forth, all you really need to do is stimulate the senses, which often remember what the mind forgets. Food is such a powerful evoker of the past that a whiff of movie popcorn or the taste of ripe strawberries dripping with juice can transport you to the past faster than the DeLorean took Michael J. Fox back to the future. Judy is the young mother who shared the stories about waking up to the smell of kolaches baking on Saturday mornings and shelling peas on the porch in a thunderstorm with her mother. She says that for many years when her entire extended family gathered on Christmas Eve, her Great-Aunt Elbe made *kuba,* a Lithuanian barley dish traditionally served with carp. A few years ago when her aunt died, the family agreed to continue serving it, not so much because it was a favorite but because it never fails to cause the stories to tumble over each other in an effort to be told.

"It's a way of remembering both Aunt Elbe and the ghost of Christmas past," Judy says. "We get to laughing about how she had a boyfriend when she was in her eighties and about her adventures learning to drive a Model T. Then somebody will say, 'The one thing about Elbe is, nobody ever left her house hungry,' and that opens the door to stories of other holidays and good times."

Like cooking, music casts a spell that inspires stories. Without exception, everyone I talked with could immediately name either a specific song or a type of music that overwhelms them with the emotions connected with a specific event or time period. When Tony began talking about 1950s rock 'n' roll, his eyes lit up at the memory of his first car, a red-and-cream 1956 Ford Crown Victoria. Polly's eyes fill with tears whenever she hears a dulcimer because it reminds her of summer nights when she darted around the front yard catching fireflies while her dad sat on the sagging front steps of their three-room house picking out "Go Tell Aunt Rhody" on the hourglass dulcimer his own father had played back in West Virginia. All it takes for my husband is the sound of Judy Collins singing the first line of "Both Sides Now," and it is 1968 all over again and he is walking a minesweep in Vietnam.

So intense is the pull of music that it can sometimes trigger memory in people whose memories have become physically impaired. One evening when I was working in the nursing home, the activities department hosted a party that included entertainment by a musical group singing old songs from the 1930s and 1940s. At the end of their performance they announced a sing-along and immediately launched into "Let Me Call You Sweetheart." I was standing beside Catherine, a small, lovely, sweet-natured lady who had suffered a stroke and could utter only one or two halting words at a time. Suddenly her face took on an almost holy radiance, and she sang two entire lines of the song as tears trickled from the corners of her eyes.

For many families the music of their country of origin, even if the family has lived in the United States for generations, serves to touch off story making. Lifestyles may change, and socioeconomic status and other commonalities may diverge, but music, which itself tells a story, reminds them of the bond that runs far deeper than any external factors ever could. Such was the case with Sheilagh. Last summer she found herself dreading the prospect of returning home for her brother's wedding. Just a few months before she had announced that she was leaving the Catholic Church to embrace her new husband's Anglican religion, and her Irish family was still reeling from the shock. "At first it was just as awkward and awful as I'd expected," she recalls of the trip. "In fact, I almost left before the reception. But then the band began to play the old ceilli tunes, and we danced and laughed and told the old stories and reminded ourselves that we're still family in spite of it all. It did not make their disappointment go away, of course, but the dear music was there like a balm for the soul."

Sometimes the lure of the past becomes so intense that it requires far more than sensory triggers to satisfy it. The ache to feel the home ground beneath our feet again, to fill our souls with the people and the places that have shaped us, is so intense that nothing will do but for us to physically return to where we or our forebears have been. Every year we make these pilgrimages by the millions—to Ireland, to our class reunions and childhood homes, to the restaurants we proposed in and the hideaway cemeteries where our ancestors lay buried. We go in hopes of recapturing something that has been lost, to find closure and/or meaning to our life story and, very often, to pass on that story to our children and our grandchildren.

In 1973, before we had our kids, my husband and I made such a journey to Ireland. We searched out a tiny greengrocer's shop on Barrack Street in the city of Cork. There, with the same portrait of my grandfather that hangs in my dining room gazing down at us from the wall, we sat in the back room of the sad, dusty shop where he was born and shared stories with his sister and brother over the same soda bread and tea we knew so well from home. A week later we traveled west to my grandmother's home in Newport, County Mayo. Every one of her brothers and sisters had died, but we found a nephew who talked of my grandmother as though she had left Ireland last week instead of fifty years ago. If I had not already been a believer in the power of story, hearing him talk with such familiarity of the Aunt Katie he had never met would surely have made me a convert.

Outside Resources
While mining your family mementos, souvenirs, foods and traditions will certainly uncover a rich vein of story material, do not limit your search for inspiration to the family circle. Movies, novels, TV shows, spiritual books and readings, as well as children's stories, can bring

long-forgotten memories drifting up from your subconscious. Almost every parent has had the experience of reading a child a bedtime story and watching in wonder as he related the fictional event to something that happened in his own life. That's why many parents deliberately seek out stories covering specific themes, such as death or divorce, to help their children talk about difficult feelings. When we moved to our present house nine years ago, Caitie was three and not at all sure she thought leaving the only home she had ever known was a good idea. To help her make a smooth transition, we read her (at least 347 times) Shirley Hughes's charming, upbeat book *Moving Molly* and told her stories about other moves we had made and about times we had thought a new experience would be scary, only to discover that scary things can actually turn out to be wonderful adventures. As our own moving story unfolded, we were also able to relate it to scenes from the book.

"Look at that backyard," I said to her after the movers had gone and we were standing in the new family room looking out at the wild, overgrown gardens. "It's just like Molly's, isn't it?"

"Yes," she replied thoughtfully, "and maybe I'll find friends in it just like Molly did."

The stories families read together are like fine metallic threads that weave themselves into the cloth of family life. Though they spring from the imaginations of creative writers, they are glints of pure gold when they actually become part of *your* family's story. It has been years since I last read Margaret Wise Brown's classic *Goodnight Moon* to a child, yet every once in a while, especially when we come home late at night and all go up to bed at the same time, one of us will spontaneously say, "Goodnight spoon, goodnight mush," and somebody else will respond, "Goodnight to the old lady whispering 'hush.' " In our family we also have a tendency to refer to the national anthem as the "Dawnzerly Light Song" because of Beverly Cleary's quirky character Ramona Quimby, whom I loved as a child and met again with Moira and Caitie. Ramona had misunderstood the lyrics.

The other day, as Moira was sorting and packing her treasured childhood books in preparation for moving into her first apartment, she mentioned that one evening at the dorm she and her college roommates had been reminiscing about their favorite childhood stories. To their mutual delight, she and Betsy discovered that they both cut their teeth on the Cleary books. Before long, to the complete bafflement of their other two roommates, they began telling each other Ramona stories. "Remember when Ramona broke the egg on her head?"

"Remember when her cat Picky-Picky died?"

"Remember how she had to stay at Howie's grandma's while her mom worked?"

Telling the stories was much more than a diversion. It was a bonding experience, a way to say, "We came from different places and backgrounds, but here in these stories, which we both love, our life stories connect." I felt that same instant rush of intimacy when I discovered that my own friend Betsy had been reading Maude Hart Lovelace's Betsy, Tacy and Tib books in a house newly planted next to a daisy field in Illinois the very same years that I was devouring them in an old inner-city house in south Akron. If books can bond friendships, imagine what they can do for family relationships![4]

Reading stories aloud, whether fairy tales, classics or sci-fi thrillers, also develops "story language." The language of story is fuller, richer and deeper than the language we use to communicate in everyday life. Those who have not grown up with stories do not always make the differentiation. Small children whose parents read to them regularly, however, pick up on it at once. When you ask them to tell you a story, they may begin "Once upon a time" and end with "And they lived happily ever after." When Moira was small, she would often tell me stories about what had happened at preschool, using such story phrases as "she said, excitedly." It is not just the kids who learn the ways of storytelling from reading aloud—the adult reader quickly learns the need for voice inflection, drama and sound effects to keep an audience awake and interested.

As spiritual seekers, we naturally gravitate to what author Madeleine L'Engle calls the world's oldest storybook—the Bible. Whether your religious background leads you to accept biblical stories as being literally true or as containing essential truths, the Bible is the ultimate sourcebook for material covering any aspect of human behavior and emotion. To make biblical events and people spring to life for your family, try a novelization of a Bible story such as *The Book of God: The Bible as a Novel* by Walter Wangerin or *Two from Galilee* by Marjorie Holmes. A novelization provides scope and immediacy. It grabs you by the heart strings and makes you care deeply about familiar characters who may not have seemed real before. All of us come to story seeking a grain of truth that is relevant to our lives, and very often we find it, not as much in the story itself as in our *response* to it. A story that makes us feel nothing teaches us nothing. The energy of biblical storytelling comes from the fire it ignites in the imagination and in the soul.[5]

Story Games

As we have seen, storytelling holds the power to do magnificent things. You can use it to shape identity, pass on beliefs and values, heal broken hearts and relationships, proclaim the presence of God, encourage creativity and language skills in children, revere the elderly, capture the past and help your family connect. But you can also use it with no other agenda than to just play together. Fun brings its own benefits, especially when you forget about trying to attain them and simply abandon yourself to the frivolity of the moment.

You may find that you are so good at storytelling that you want to try your hand at making up a story of your own. Classic favorites such as *Alice in Wonderland, The Tale of Peter Rabbit* and *Watership Down* got their start as stories told to children. But if you are not ready to get quite *that* creative, why not try retelling a folk tale or a myth? The library is full of resources containing simple, fun stories that are easy to learn and retell to the delight of a mixed group of ages and interests. You may want to begin with a story from your own cultural heritage and then move on to explore some from other lands. Caroline, a kindergarten teacher, discovered a passion for storytelling when she needed to entertain her kids on a long, unexpected layover at the Atlanta airport on the way home from a long, hot week of trekking around Florida's many theme parks. Out of desperation she began retelling such old chestnuts as "Little Red Riding Hood" and "Cinderella." Almost immediately the fighting stopped, the snack requests dwindled and nobody whined, "When are we getting on the plane?"

"It started a whole thing going," she says. "Now, every so often, I'll take the time to learn a new story. Once I have it down pat, I make a big deal out of it. I might plan a special meal that picks up the theme, or maybe we'll make something. One time I did a Japanese story about a thousand paper cranes and we did origami. The kids love it and so does my husband. One of the best times was last August during the Perseid meteor showers. We sat out on a blanket in the backyard watching for meteors, and I told the Greek legend of Perseus."

Another way to play with storytelling, especially on car trips or around the campfire, is to begin a round-robin story. One person sets the scene, introduces the characters, sets up the problem, and then leaves it for someone else to continue. The next storyteller picks up the yarn and continues until he has either created a cliffhanger or has gotten himself hopelessly tangled in his own plot. Then he stops and allows another teller to continue the tale. Some families like to pass around an object such as a special stone or stick. Whoever holds the story stone is the teller, and nobody else may speak until the stone is passed. When I was working at the nursing home, I once started a round robin with a black-and-white photo of a mysterious old house with broken windows that must have belonged to the Addams family.

Just for fun, I gathered a group of mentally sharp people from the assisted living building and began by passing around the picture for everyone to study. Then I started a crazy tale about an eccentric old woman named Lilac Tatterlace who kept a beehive in the front parlor. Unlike ordinary bees, Lilac's buzzers were a little-known strain of purple bee she had smuggled into the country from Tasmania for their magical, lavender-scented honey. A single dose of it was known to cure dropsy, ague, humours, catarrh and a host of other nineteenth-century maladies. Every night by the light of a single candle she would play her wheezy piano. The bees would waft out of the hive and begin a graceful precision aerial ballet to the tune of "Clair de Lune." One evening while the bees were dancing, a mad scientist named Aloyious J. Finestine, who lived next door and had ears like radar (thanks to an unfortunate explosion in his basement la-*bore*-a-tory), picked up the bees' eerie, high-pitched hum and realized that something very strange was going on in his neighbor's spooky old house. He crept stealthily through the wisteria on the front porch and peered in the window. Seeing the deep purple bees pirouetting around the parlor, he gasped in horror. Did Lilac Tatterlace not realize that Tasmanian purple predator bees had the power to . . .

I stopped and let somebody else run with it. Round and round the circle the story bounced like a hard rubber ball, flying crazily in every direction, skittering into odd corners and finally coming to rest at an ending that left us all limp with laughter. Reluctantly, I returned to my office to cries of "That was fun" and "Let's do it again sometime!"

You do not need a picture or an object to get a round robin going, but it helps at the beginning. Kids attuned to TV and videos tend to be highly visual and can have trouble creating a story without something concrete in front of them. The trick is to be imaginative, not worry about how wacky the plot gets and just have fun with it.

Another playful way to introduce your family to creative storytelling is through a commercial card game, Once upon a Time, published by Atlas Games. It is a visually beautiful, ingeniously imaginative way for the entire family to create a story together based on familiar elements from fairy tales. Only rudimentary reading skills are necessary, so even young children can play. Yet it is challenging enough to hook older kids and adults. The game consists of 112 Once upon a Time storytelling cards and 56 Happily Ever After cards. The person who goes first, the storyteller, creates an original story using the elements depicted on the cards she is dealt and attempts to guide the tale's events toward her own ending. Meanwhile, her opponents are busy using the story elements on their own cards to interrupt her and become the new storyteller. The winner is the first player to play out all his cards and end with a Happily Ever After card. I like this game very much because it provides beginning storytellers with prompts and structure and helps visually oriented children focus. It is pocket-size and great to carry along for those inevitable times when kids get restless.

The Nostalgia Trap

Sacred storytelling is meant to be a celebration of life, a thanksgiving for earthly gifts both large and small, and a hymn of praise to the Creator who showers them on us every day in glorious abundance. When we succumb to its pleasures, we step out of real time and into "God time," where we forget the tyranny of the clock and our own egocentricities, concentrating on the ecstasy of being with those we love. Sharing the small events of the present and playing with stories with a sense of childlike wonder and innocence also keeps us from falling into nostalgia, one of the worst traps of *un*holy storytelling.

As a storyteller, you are charged with a sacred mission—remembering the past and keeping it alive. But you are *not* charged to live in it. When storytelling lapses into nostalgia and sentimentality, it restructures the past by painting it such a rosy hue that its true colors, which are pure enough in their own truth, can no longer shine. It also tempts you to yearn so deeply for what is gone that today's gifts slip by unnoticed until they also become part of history. We have all known people who moan and groan about how terrible things are now. After five years pass, they refer back to the very same period they had earlier lamented as "the good old days." We can only pity them, since in the end they will have enjoyed so few authentic moments.

The difference between waxing nostalgic and savoring the past is the difference between talking about having a party and actually having one. You can sit around hashing over old times until you convince yourself that nothing will ever again be as good as the way it used to be, or you can turn on the music and tell the old stories while you are caught up in the sublime joy of dancing a new one. When Jeannie and Garrett had their family reunion last summer, the relatives came with old stories and old photos, but also with baseball mitts, badminton sets, green bean casseroles and jugs of lemonade. And there on the ball diamond, over the net, and around the picnic tables a miracle took place. The past and present converged, and—lo!—a new story was born.

Things to Talk About

1. How mindful are you of small graces? What do you think gets in the way? How can you become more aware of small pleasures?

2. How does being mindful help you to grow spiritually? What is it

that you most want to memorize as Jose Hobday memorized the land and the sight of the Sleeping Ute?

3. How does playing become praying?

Things to Do Right Now

1. Tell your family a story of something you experienced today. Remember, the magnitude of the event is far less important than the magnitude of your awe and gratitude.

2. Use a memory trigger, such as food, souvenirs, music or a short trip, to help you remember stories of the past.

3. Turn off the TV and read aloud as a family. Let everyone help choose the book.

4. Play a storytelling game. You can use one of the ones mentioned above, or you can make up one of your own. Sit around a campfire or fireplace, or on the porch at night, and let your imagination run wild.

Nine

Marking the Moments
The Link Between Ritual & Storytelling

I T WAS EARLY MORNING, BUT ALREADY THE DESERT HEAT BURNED THROUGH the soles of my sandals as I climbed the small hill east of the Mission of San Xavier (hauv-e-air) Del Bac, south of Tucson. Eric paused, looked down at the old white church rising ghostlike out of the sand, snapped a picture and continued climbing. We did not—could not—speak. On the reservation of the Tohono O'Odham Indians, beauty and squalor share squatter's rights. It stuns you into silence.

If I were to dream of that July day, it would be in three colors: the tan of the desert floor, the blue of the vast sky, and the alabaster white of the church. I would hear one sound: the haunting keen of the Indian flute drifting over the loudspeaker system erected at the souvenir shops across the road. I know, of course, that the purpose of this music is crassly commercial, yet the memory of it fills me with a strange amalgam of melancholy and hope that feels, even now, like a benediction.

Earlier we had toured the church itself, filing quietly past the statue of Saint Francis (San Francisco) lying beneath a collection of small embroidered coverlets. Every day parishioners and pilgrims make their way down the aisle in a slow, steady stream to pin tiny golden charms in the shape of hands, feet, arms and legs to the cloths as tokens of gratitude for healing. The natives call the charms *milagros* and accompany them with heartfelt notes to the saint carefully composed in English or Spanish. In the sense that it is foreign to me, it is a strange ritual. Yet it touches me profoundly, not only because of what it says about faith but also for what it says about the people who perform it.

Like all rituals, the ritual of the *milagros* tells the story of the people who embrace it. As we slowly made our way past the reposing statue of Saint Francis, a blond, blue-eyed young couple ahead of us in line gazed down at the plaster figure, laden as it was with charms and notes written on the kind of lined notebook paper children use in school, and shuddered ever so slightly. "It's so bizarre," the wife whispered.

"Almost pagan," her husband agreed, a touch too loudly.

Since I have no way of knowing where that attractive young couple came from, what they believed in or what gave them a sense of meaning and fulfillment, I can only surmise. Maybe they sip Communion wine from tiny individual cups in the pews of a plain, white-steepled church in Iowa on Sunday mornings. Or make snowmen with their children in a backyard in Wisconsin and sing them the "Itsy Bitsy Spider" song before tucking them into bed. Almost certainly they stuff a turkey on Thanksgiving, light candles on their birthday cakes, sing "Auld Lang Syne" on New Year's Eve and celebrate the Fourth of July in an explosion of skyrockets and Roman candles.

Wherever they come from or whatever they do, I doubt very much that they were thinking about these quintessential American traditions and the gaping holes that would be left in their story lives if they were abruptly stripped away. They were fixated on how different, and therefore how unacceptable, it is to carry on a personal, emotional, perhaps even sentimental relationship with a saint who had been a mere mortal himself centuries before. But by not remembering their own symbolic acts—*acts that are not shared by all people everywhere*—they failed to see that it is through our most cherished rituals that each of us, with passion, honesty, creativity, love and reverence, gives voice to the melody of the spirit of our people and the individual music of our own souls. Each time ritual becomes story, we sing our own unique song. But it is only when we join our song with the songs of others, equally unique, that the many voices of the family of humankind rise in a celebration of unity and diversity.

Whether you are consciously aware of it or not, your family is already carrying out many, many rituals that give shape and substance to the stories you tell. Some of them are indigenous to the culture, others are peculiar to your own clan, but all of them fall into five general, sometimes overlapping, categories: everyday activities, family traditions, holiday celebrations, life-cycle observances and lifestyle markers.

Everyday activities include the way you greet and say goodby to one another, Monday-night grocery shopping, grace before meals, the pizza you order for dinner on Fridays, and the way you always set the timer on the coffeemaker before you go to bed because you love the way the house smells in the morning when the aroma of freshly brewed Italian roast wafts up the stairs. More than likely these actions are so intrinsic to the fabric of your life that you are scarcely aware of them, even though they speak volumes about who you are, what matters to you, how your family relates to one another, and what you fear and dream. If your listener happens to share your everyday rituals or does not need to stretch her imagination too far to assimilate them, they become the salt of your stories, adding taste and interest, but not jolting the senses. But if you are an Orthodox Jew who keeps kosher and lives in the city and if your listener is a Presbyterian who lives on a two-hundred-acre dairy farm, suddenly these everyday rituals are no longer common salt but cayenne and cardamom, turmeric and marjoram—exotic and unusual. Yet whether they are plain or unusual really does not matter because the details of ritual are always the defining elements of story. Without salt, without spice, the story is flat and bland because there is nothing that speaks to either the senses or the soul.

Much more obvious than everyday rituals are your family traditions and holiday observances, since they happen less frequently and can assume an almost magical quality. Observances include the time-honored fishing trip to Canada the second week of July, the custom of passing down family names and the annual trek to the woods to chop down your own Christmas tree. These types of rituals give rise to your family's most cherished memories and stories, but they can also cause the most friction among family members. As they grow up, move away and establish families of their own, they may balk at the rigidity of old expectations, which require adaptation to survive.

Life-cycle observances happen even less frequently than holiday celebrations. They are the rites that (1) mark your milestone events, (2) guide you through the transition from one state of being or one stage of life into another and (3) provide the basis for your most essential stories. They include births, baptisms, confirmations, graduations, engagements, weddings, wakes and funerals. Because they are among the most solemn and meaningful acts of your life, they often give rise to deep and sometimes conflicting emotions. The bride wants her beloved father to walk her down the aisle and "give her away" in marriage, but struggles with the concept of being owned and being symbolically transferred from one man's authority to another's. The family wants to honor their mother's desire for cremation, but laments the fact that there will be no calling hours at the funeral home as there were when their father died. Life-cycle rituals require serious thought, and often compromise and/or acceptance, because they make a major impact on the family's story of itself.

The rituals that mark lifestyle changes are the ones that people tend to adapt and personalize. Their ritualistic nature centers more on the fact of the observance itself than it does on the actual means of commemoration. When Dad is promoted to national sales manager, the family may celebrate over dinner at a favorite seafood restaurant. A year later, when Mom makes partner at the law firm, they might choose to mark it with a weekend trip to a nearby resort. In both instances they observe the honor but feel unconfined in their means of expression. Other change-of-lifestyle observances include house-warmings, celebrations of new jobs or awards, bon voyage parties and parties commemorating newly licensed drivers. Whether they happen once or numerous times, these rituals herald your achievements and/or celebrate your ability to bring about bold new changes. And they create stories that you tell and retell long after the occasion has past.

Rituals and Reflection

Whether large or small, personal or familial, rituals imbue your life with structure, continuity and meaning. Their power lies in the fact that they simultaneously encompass both constancy and transformation. The kiss you give your spouse as you fly out the door to work in the morning is a constant, one of literally thousands of goodby kisses in a lifetime. They affix you firmly in the present and simultaneously acknowledge your passage from the comfort of home to the demands of the larger world. The same is true of the bedtime story you read your child. As you automatically reach for the well-thumbed storybook, you know that not only will you be reaching for it tomorrow and the next night, but bedtime stories will continue to be read as long as there are parents and children and the moon rises faithfully in the night sky. Meanwhile, in the act of turning the pages, you mark the transition from wakefulness to sleep. So too the ritual of the *milagros* reflects both the abiding faith of the natives in the power of Saint Francis Xavier to intercede on their behalf and in their transformation from illness to health.

There is great comfort in ritual. Like a story that wraps itself around you in a warm cocoon of words, ritual brings familiarity to the abyss of the unknown. After the long, lingering death of her husband from cancer, forty-nine-year-old Alicia went back to college and on a whim signed up to spend a semester studying in China's Shanxi Province. Her eyes glistening with tears, she recalls the sweet solace of trimming a Christmas tree in a cold cement dormitory building with her fellow American and European students, using whatever was at hand to make decorations. Not long after they plugged in the only strand of lights they had been able to find, a group of Chinese friends arrived with a roasted turkey because they had heard that many Westerners eat turkey during the winter holidays. Sharing the familiar rituals with a new, young "family" gathered from all over the world during the most difficult Christmas of her life, Alicia created an unforgettable celebration and a poignant tale that lies nestled at the bottom of her story bag like treasure.

In earlier chapters we saw that ritual and storytelling are closely tied, each one feeding and sustaining the other. As you begin to claim the storytelling tradition for your family, it is important to consider what kinds of rituals you perform, what they mean, and how significant these acts are to the overall pattern and texture of your life. If you feel a strong pull to reclaim rituals you abandoned in the busyness of seeking your fortune, you may be interested in identity maintenance.

Julie had been brought up in the Episcopal Church, but religion began to seem irrelevant after she left home to attend college in another state. She was married in the church because her parents expected it and also, she says, wincing a little, because the spectacular stained-glass windows made an ideal backdrop for the carefully choreographed pictures in her wedding album. Once she ran out the church's red doors through a crowd of well-wishers with her new husband, himself a lapsed Methodist, she never went back—until now, when she returns almost daily in her thoughts. At forty-four she feels a vague, unsettled yearning for liturgy. "Sometimes I'll be cleaning up the breakfast dishes, and the house is so quiet with everyone gone, and the sun will come slanting in through the kitchen window, and all of a sudden I'll find myself singing the Te Deum," she says. "It's like it's calling to me from somewhere far away."[1]

Liz spoke of a longing to reclaim her roots in her German culture. Born near West Berlin, she immigrated to the United States with her parents and older brother when she was three years old. The family discovered a vibrant German community in Columbus, Ohio, and settled in. After the first months of struggle, the family continued to live pretty much the same lifestyle they had enjoyed an ocean away. As a child, Liz reveled in the rich foods, music, language and holiday rituals of her homeland, which gave rhythm and warm familiarity to her life. But for high school she transferred out of her neighborhood school system to a fashionable private academy attended by few, if any, immigrants. Then she began to turn her back on her heritage.

"It all started with sandwiches," she says, laughing ruefully. "The very first day at lunch in the school cafeteria, the rest of the kids unpacked their tuna fish on white bread and there I was with these huge bratwurst smothered in sauerkraut on black bread. It was so embarrassing I wanted to crawl under the table and die. I decided right then and there that I'd rather starve than show up with those things. From then on, my goal was to out-American the Americans."

Having reached her late thirties, with her two teenage sons plugged into rap music and littering her suburban family room with cheese curls and soda cans, Liz finds her thoughts straying to the Oktoberfest she used to love at the local German club her parents still belong to, folk dances and potato salad made with hot bacon grease and vinegar. Snatches of the language she eschewed in high school drift back to her, and she feels a sadness that her children consider Germany as far removed from their lives as Mars. She vows to change that and prays that it is not too late to reach the tall, gangly boys in the baggy shorts who laughed when she told them the story of the sandwiches and said, "Well *duh,* Mom," which (as every parent of 90s children well knows) loosely translated means, "What could you expect when you turned up with food as weird as that?"

Like many people in or approaching midlife, both Julie and Liz are beginning to realize that time, family and authenticity are gifts too precious to be squandered. They want to take stock, discern their successes and failures, shed old baggage and determine exactly what they will bring with them on the journey into the second half of life. Typically, midlife is characterized by the desire to emerge as a strong individualist, sure of purpose and independent of societal definitions of what is successful, trendy or appropriate. Both women are discovering that in order to go forward, it is often necessary to momentarily take a step back and reclaim the past.

If your life is already rich with ritual, you may realize that you perform much of it in a daze, going through the motions because you always have or because it is expected without really considering what any of it means and whether or not it is significant to you now. Rituals give your life meaning only when you attribute meaning to them. Two people can perform the same act; for one it is a mindful, significant experience, while to the other it has as much importance as a sneeze. Often I have sat in church waiting for the service to begin and have watched people come down the aisle, stop before a pew and perform a funny little bob at the knees while their eyes scan the congregation for people they know. If asked, I am sure they would call the bob a genuflection, but their minds are clearly so far from God that, in that instance at least, they have managed to render meaningless an act of profound reverence. If you are like many of the people I spoke with, however, your time-honored traditions *do* have meaning for you. But in order to carry them out with a greater depth of consciousness and understanding, it is essential to reflect on that meaning both historically and in the context of your present life. Such was the case with Ethan, who spoke with intensity about his family's tradition of involvement with the county fair.

Ever since he was a small child, the county fair in August crowned the family's entire year. He and his father showed their prize cattle, his sister her horses, and his mother her dahlias, pies, needlework and antiques. Twenty years after moving away from home, he still spends every night of fair week at the fairgrounds, even though he is no longer an exhibitor and works as a stockbroker for one of the nation's largest brokerage firms. His wife, Karen, is an ER nurse at a large metropolitan hospital who considers her microwave her most valuable appliance. They live in a sprawling suburban development of look-alike four-bedroom colonial houses ten miles from the family farm. Their children play Little League baseball and soccer and have no interest in 4-H. On the surface at least, it would seem that the county fair would be as relevant to this family as a barn raising or a quilting bee. But Ethan does not see it that way.

"Ten years ago if you'd have asked me why we still identify so strongly with the fair, I'd have said it's because we're addicted to the food," he said with a grin. "Also, when my parents were alive it was kind of expected. But the truth is, it goes much deeper than that. Even though I no longer participate in it on a day-to-day basis, the agricultural life of this community is in my blood and bones. My family's been part of it for 150 years, so it's been bred into me. The older I get, the more I feel a need to hang on to a little piece of it. The development around here is exploding. If it keeps up at this rate, we're going to be one massive subdivision in twenty years. Anymore, every farm that's razed by the bulldozers seems like another death to me, and every year that we still walk down that midway is one more reprieve."

Sometimes the process of reflecting on our rituals reveals obvious gaps, places where we fail to mark transitions in ways that are satisfying to our souls. When that happens, it becomes necessary to devise new rituals by carefully considering what we believe and what symbolic actions best give voice to the unsung songs of our hearts. Families spoke about devising their own rituals to celebrate the anniversary of their children's adoptions, their daughter's emergence into young womanhood, and the deaths of beloved pets. Psychologist Elaine Wynne shared a ritual her family devised when her children turned eighteen to mark their passage from childhood to adulthood. Because she is a professional storyteller and also uses storytelling as a therapeutic technique, it is not surprising that the ritual centers on family stories.

Some months before the celebration, the child who is making the transition is asked to choose two adult guides, one male and one female, to help steer the family through the process. On the designated day, the parents, the child and the guides sit down together and tell each other the stories of the child's life divided into three time frames: conception to age six, ages six to twelve, and ages twelve to eighteen. Typically, the next four or five hours are punctuated by moments of exhilaration, sadness and even anger, as differing points of view emerge. But finally the story bag is depleted, and everyone sits for a time in silence, reflecting on what has been said. Then the child is told that she is ready to enter the passageway of choosing to be an adult, but that the decision to do so is hers alone. Afterward friends and family gather for a huge party to surround the young person with love and support as she enters a new phase of her life. Both parents and child must be gentle with themselves in the days that follow the celebration, Wynne cautions, because though the overall result is one of deep healing, the ritual triggers the *necessary* sadness that comes with the passing of childhood.

"The reason I did this," she says, "is that in my practice I see so many people in their forties who still have so much anguish about the past. A lot of it is because they never really leave, either because their parents won't let them or because leavetaking is so painful."

Rituals do not have to be as formal and as encompassing as Wynne's. Equally satisfying are small rituals like the one Karen's family devised to celebrate their house's birthday. Each year on the anniversary of the date they moved into the dream house they built five years ago, they celebrate with a cake and a special birthday present. "We have a family meeting and vote on buying something special for the house that we'll all enjoy. The size of the gift depends on our finances," Karen laughs. "The first year we were broke, but the cable TV company was running a special, so we got the house hooked up to basic cable. This year we're extending the deck. By that I mean with our own labor."

To some people the idea of having a birthday party for a house may seem odd, but Karen explains that it is less about the house itself and more about what the house symbolizes—the realization of a dream and the closeness of the family it shelters. "We built this to be our 'forever house,' " she says. "It's where we want to make all of our memories, so it's important to us to mark the day we first began to live here."

Go with the Flow

Aside from the fact that Karen's house ritual bears her family's unique stamp and expresses something that they value enormously, it is also noteworthy because it exemplifies how rituals can maintain a level of flexibility without losing their significance. The family gauges the size of their celebration in terms of their bank account, but even in lean years manages to carry out their original intention. When rituals become so rigid that they extract more than can be comfortably given, they are no longer a celebration but a form of enslavement.

Ritual should never be solely contingent on money or things, but on the values of the participants.

Sometimes as circumstances change and families grow, rituals that once held great significance no longer seem meaningful. If a ritual you have been following for years no longer tells your story, expresses your beliefs and values, and fills you with a sense of continuity and satisfaction, it may need modification. This is also true of rituals that cannot be continued due to factors beyond your control, such as aging, illness or the death of a family member. Change is always scary, because it implies a loss of history and stability. But rather than simply abandoning rituals, we can often update them in light of present circumstances. Rather than mourn the fact that Aunt Nora is too arthritic to make the Christmas fruitcakes that even fruitcake haters love, the rest of the family can pitch in on baking day, make a party of it, and allow Aunt Nora be the overseer. To make such changes with grace requires a willingness to be open, surrendering preconceived ideas of the way things "must" be or "should" be and talking openly and lovingly with family members to create traditions that will ultimately prove just as satisfying as, or even more satisfying than, the old ones.

After Jessica's father died a few years ago, the entire family went into a tailspin as each holiday rolled around. For as long as they could remember, Grandpa's sprawling white house by the lake had been the setting for every family gathering, and his presence the hub on which the entire wheel turned. Forming new holiday traditions proved painful, especially that first year when not all family members embraced them at the same pace. Four years after her father's death, the family is starting to feel comfortable with the new ways of celebration. As Jessica learned through trial and error, it is essential that each family member is allowed to progress at an individual rate, is part of the decision-making, and understands that creating meaningful rituals is a *process* that will probably include a few mistakes.

The first Thanksgiving following her dad's death, the family invited some close friends to their home for dinner. While this worked well for the parents and their two daughters, it did not work well at all for their son. He felt that tradition was being thrown to the four winds.

The next year Jessica and her husband took his feelings into account by keeping the celebration strictly family, which opened the door to storytelling about their grandfather and past holidays. This reminiscing proved to be the missing component for their son. "The important thing is not to get stuck in the past," Jessica says. "I told the kids right from the start that Grandpa wouldn't want us sitting around with long faces. We need to move forward and celebrate life with the same gusto he did, because his enthusiasm for life was his legacy to us."

Another family experienced a difficult time letting go of a ritual that began when their children were very small. Every Christmas Eve the kids would put on their pajamas and their mom, Claudia, would make special hot cocoa with candy-cane swizzle sticks. Then the entire family would watch *Christmas Eve on Sesame Street,* a warm, funny, engaging video about the meaning of Christmas. The only problem was that she persisted with it long after the kids had outgrown it. "I couldn't give it up," she admits. "My husband and I still liked it as adults, so we couldn't see why the kids didn't. But by pushing it so hard and long we took away the magic. Now they hate it, and all the warm memories are history."

In retrospect, Claudia realizes that it was the closeness and the delicious sense of expectation and excitement that the video engendered that she loved, not the video itself. She feels now that it would have been far wiser to have substituted another activity that would have brought about the same benefits, while acknowledging the fact that the children were growing up and moving into a new stage of maturation.

The fluidity of ritual allows you to change, mold and adapt the old ways of doing things to fit your present lifestyle, but it does not demand perfection in order to be successful. When you approach ritual with a sense of humor, any deviations from the ideal can actually enrich your story life. Monica and Charlie, who were married four years ago at a formal concelebrated Mass in a cavernous, ornate cathedral, delight in showing their wedding video to unsuspecting viewers. As the large wedding party moves slowly and elegantly down the long, white runner, the tiny red-haired flower girl suddenly twirls in her long periwinkle gown, flashes a huge grin to the pews at her right and calls out, "Hi, Grandma! See my flowers? Neat, huh?"

Some couples would have viewed the flower girl's action as a major disaster. But the video shows Charlie and Monica sharing a delighted grin before taking their places at the altar. "When you have a three-year-old in the wedding, you have to be ready for anything," Monica says. "We loved it. Kelly's seven now, and she even tells the story herself. It'll go down in family history."

When you are open to the fluidity of ritual, you can also benefit from one of its most mysterious and deeply gratifying characteristics—its ability not only to announce change but to actually effect it. Anne, who earlier shared the story of how the death of her grandmother Lena's fiancé enabled her to get through the pain of her own messy divorce, shared another story about how her sisters and her best friend helped her mark her difficult, involuntary passage from wife to single mother. "After the divorce we had to sell our home, so the kids and I moved into an apartment," she explains. "It was the first time I'd ever lived alone, and I was feeling pretty shaky and unsure of myself, so my sisters and my best friend got together and gave me a shower. My sisters came three hundred miles to do this, if you can believe it. Anyway, the guests were instructed to bring the 'tools' I would need in my new life. I got the obvious wrenches and pliers and screwdrivers, but I also got bubble bath and perfume, books, a journal and even the beginnings of a small savings account. But the best gift of all was a beautifully polished pink stone shaped like a heart that fit in the palm of my hand to remind me that I can be soft and strong at the same time."

Anne's misgivings remained after the party, of course, but the support her friends and family had shown her, as well as the tangible and highly symbolic "tools" they left behind, gradually began to make her feel more confident. The internal shift came about as a direct result of the fact that they had honored her as a capable, confident, secure woman who was trying to emerge from the person of the wounded one.

When you "go with the flow" and allow for fluidity in ritual making, you can tap into the power of story to guide you in forming new or adapted rituals that more meaningfully express your family's beliefs. Hidden inside each family story (especially the ones you tell most often) are clues that can tell you much about what is really most precious to you. Sometimes, if you pay attention, you may even find a few surprises, as Jennie's family did when they wrestled with the problem of how to celebrate Easter.

No matter what they chose to do, whether hosting the family gathering at their house after church or going to dinner at another family member's home, the day invariably seemed a little flat, despite their assertion that being with extended family was what mattered most to them. One evening shortly after New Year's Day they were sitting around the dinner table talking about where to go on vacation that summer and telling stories of past vacations, when Jennie came to a startling realization. "The kids were telling a story about the time they were swimming in a hotel pool in North Carolina and mistook a little girl from Hawaii for their cousin Melissa. They were laughing about it and remembering how much fun they'd had with her, when suddenly it struck me: *Who says we can only go on vacation in the summer?*" she says.

Though a little leery about breaking tradition, spending a major holiday apart from the aunts and uncles, and taking their one and only vacation so early in the year, Jennie's family opted to spend that Easter on Sanibel Island. On Easter morning they were returning to their oceanfront condo after attending a sunrise service on the beach when they saw a sight that has come to symbolize for them resurrection, freedom and the importance of following your own heart. "It was low tide, and there was this whole mass of gigantic pink birds standing so still they looked like lawn ornaments," Jennie says. "They kind of reminded me of herons with their long, gangly legs. We stopped and watched for a second. Then one of them started raising his head up and down, and all of a sudden, *whoosh!* They took off in an enormous flash of brilliant rose feathers. It was the most fantastic thing I've ever seen."

The trip to Sanibel and the sight of the roseate spoonbills taking flight reiterated what their stories had already told them. Though they dearly love their extended family and want to spend most holidays with them, deep down they believe that Easter is a time of new beginning, a time for resurrection and renewal. For a family who finds its greatest joy and rejuvenation in travel, an Easter journey is the ideal answer to the call of the spirit and the creation of a story that expresses identity.

Ritual and Morality

Carl A. Hammerschlag, a psychiatrist who works with the people of the Hopi Indian nation in Arizona, says, "We can return to a life of morality through telling and listening to stories, through experiencing genuine awe, through participating in rituals and ceremonies."[2] Reading that statement was like finding the missing piece of the jigsaw puzzle. Somewhere in the fuzzy recesses of my mind was already lurking the notion that storytelling and ritual had a definite link to morality aside from the obvious use of storytelling to pass along values. But I had not been able to put it into words. Immediately I was reminded of Jennie's family and the vacation stories that had led them to follow their hearts and make a change.

As I thought about their wonder at the sight of God's glorious creation and the ritual of their yearly trip at Easter, I realized that they do not take those trips out of a sense of duty or to impress the neighbors, or even in search of hedonistic pleasures, although they certainly do have a great deal of fun. Rather, they take them to carve out a special time to delight in each other's company, to be enthralled by the many splendors of the earth and to find physical, emotional and spiritual renewal. The trips underscore everything that gives their lives meaning and enhance that sense of meaning in a symbolic way.

Without meaning we cannot achieve true morality. We can obey the laws of the land out of a sense of fear or obligation while lacking a desire to make the world a better place. Service, kindness, charity, empathy, honesty, fidelity—all the hallmarks of the truly moral person—would be conspicuously absent because there would no longer be any reason for them to exist. In an amoral world, crime, substance abuse and acts of unspeakable inhumanity burgeon because everyone is driven by the same sense of alienation and emptiness. Without a strong connection to family and friends, work that fulfills us and makes a contribution to society, a sense of childlike wonder, and a belief in something greater than ourselves, we become angry, apathetic and cynical. To live a moral life and to help our children live one too it is essential that we return to the basics and honor once again our families, the changing of the seasons, the milestone events of our lives, the glories of the universe, and our relationship with the Divine. One of the most definitive ways we can do that is by carrying out our rituals and by telling our stories right here, today, in the midst of a world that sometimes seems to be spinning out of control.[3]

As Mary Pipher says in her wonderful book *The Shelter of Each Other: Rebuilding Our Families,* "The best resource against the world's stupidity, meanness and despair is simply telling the truth with all its ambiguity and complexity. We can all make a difference simply by sharing our stories with real people in real times and places."[4]

It is late on an early summer evening as I sit in my wicker rocking chair on the screened porch with Caitie, pondering these weighty thoughts. I am tired, but too peacefully lethargic to get up and climb the stairs to bed, so we sit in the dark and lazily talk about the day just past. She plays Beethoven's "Ode to Joy" for me on her violin because she knows I love it. Then she plucks a leaf from the pot of red geraniums in the corner and gives it to me to share her pleasure in its spicy scent. Finally she launches into a long story about cheerleading camp, replete with an energetic demonstration. I laugh at her amazing ability to flip and whirl through the air and listen dreamily as the rockers of the chair seem to pick up her constant refrain, "And then, Mom, . . . and then, Mom, . . . and then, Mom . . ."

There is an ache in the small of my back from bending over the flats of pachysandra I planted by the picket fence this afternoon, but I don't mind. The annual trip to the garden store and the feel of loose, warm dirt threaded with earthworms please me deeply. This porch, finally finished, pleases me too. And so does this child. On this quiet, uneventful, amazing night in June I don't even mind that my agent has had no news about the children's novel I wrote, that the lawn needs to be mowed, that my husband will be out of town for another week or that Moira's tuition will be due in a month. It is enough that I am simply here enjoying this ritual of sitting on the porch listening to my youngest child tell me a story on a fine summer night.

And then of course I see. It is the important rituals that mark our most momentous events, but it is the small ones that, if we let them, have the power to make the ordinary sublime.

Things to Talk About

1. Has there ever been a time when a ritual eased you through a rough transition? If so, how?

2. What were the rituals of your childhood? Have you carried them on into adulthood? If not, would you like to revisit them?

3. What rituals do you perform without much thought? Does this mean that they are not meaningful to you, or are you too busy or too preoccupied to give them your full attention? What would happen if you began to live more mindfully?

4. Think of a small moment that stands out in your mind because of the satisfaction and contentment it brought you. What made it so special? How can you bring more of those same feelings into your life on a regular basis?

Things to Do Right Now

1. Make five lists. Label them everyday rituals, holiday celebrations, family traditions, life-cycle observances and lifestyle markers. Think about the rituals in your life and fill them in on the appropriate list. Then go back and consider each one individually. Does it give you pleasure? Why? Are you clinging to it out of habit when it is no longer meaningful? Can it be adapted or changed to be more meaningful?

2. Look at your lists again, only this time in terms of what can be added. Are there strong beliefs or feelings, important events or transitions that your family does not honor with rituals? How might that be changed? Have a family brainstorming session.

3. Even if you are basically happy with your rituals, work together to add a new ritual that is meaningful to the entire family. It might

be a family night when each person takes a turn choosing the menu and activity or a family activity that gives something back to the community. Whatever it is, be sure to state exactly what the ritual means and why it is important to you.

4. Ask friends and family members to share their rituals with you. Expand your family's experiences by observing or participating in rituals from another culture.

Ten

Completing
the Circle

Stories That Bond

T HE MOON, ALMOST FULL, SHINES THROUGH A CANOPY OF LEAFY TREES.
In the dark woods a twig snaps, followed by the scurrying of a small
animal through the underbrush.

Around the blazing campfire a circle of ten people sit clutching
mugs of hot coffee against the chill of a late spring evening and
watching as moonlight silvers the water of the pond they
euphemistically call "the lake."

"Remember the time Pauline and Clarice tried making homemade
angel food cake for somebody's birthday?" one of them asks.

The other nine burst out laughing. They begin to tell the story as
a group, each one adding details like rare spices to a communal
recipe, a dash of curry here, a few threads of saffron there. There is
disagreement over the number of failed attempts, but everyone agrees
that however many it was, by the time they were finished they had
enough ruined pieces to fill a galvanized washtub clear to the top.

"They hauled it over to the cabin—I think it must have been Rick's
birthday because it was in the spring—with all those crazy signs and

candles sticking out of it and . . ."

The voices rise in disagreement over whose birthday it actually was and then dissolve again in shared laughter.

In alpine regions when fog settles in and envelops the trees in a pearl-gray mist, something rare happens. A luminous ring forms in the sky opposite the sun like a halo of pure white light. Scientists call it the circle of Ullea, or the white rainbow. On that long-ago night in May, as I sat in that shining circle of storytellers listening to their laughter skip like stones across the water, I thought of it. Though I was part of their circle, it was only by virtue of my recent engagement to their brother/nephew/son. How many years would have to pass, I wondered, before I could supply the missing name or place, understand the inside jokes, or say with the impunity of an insider, "Remember the time we . . ."?

Looking back, I cannot pinpoint when it finally happened. It must have taken place gradually, rather like seeds sprouting in a garden. You look and look and see no progress, and then suddenly there is a small green seedling sprouting strong and sturdy out of the damp earth as though it were meant to grow exactly there. Since the time it opened to include me, the Kindig family circle has widened to make room for several more "outsiders." Then it again closes, a little larger and brighter than before.

Though I come from a long line of Irish storytellers, I marvel still at the differences between my two families. From my own family I learned a richness of detail and a cadence of language. But from my husband's I learned about the relationship between storytelling and intimacy.

Families who tell stories that evoke a sense of communion and belonging share one primary characteristic—respect for the physical, emotional, psychological and spiritual boundaries of their members. They admire an original thought or different point of view, are not afraid to get their feet wet in unfamiliar waters, respect one anther's privacy, and welcome friends and friends of friends and treat them *almost* like family. They invite the whole gang for dinner when they have made too much spaghetti sauce, help install the new dishwasher, offer to keep the kids so everybody gets an occasional night out, spread the word of family successes, and brush off those who have fallen flat on their faces. When one of their members occasionally acts like a perfect idiot, they tell him he is acting like a perfect idiot but love him just the same. Their stories may not be as edgy, detailed, dramatic or incisive as the ones told by other kinds of families—they may even be the storytelling equivalent of white bread and vanilla pudding—but they have smooth, round edges. Nobody gets hurt.

This kinder, gentler brand of storytelling is as comfortable as an old pair of worn and faded jeans. The fact that the stories and the humor they express seem interesting and funny primarily to the ones sharing them is precisely the point—you had to have been there. It is as though the entire body of stories, jokes, touchstones and rituals is a legacy, an heirloom as precious as the family silver or the friendship quilt made by Great-Grandma's sewing circle back in Cedar Rapids during World War I. When you realize that you are finally in on the joke, perceive all the nuances of a gesture or an expression, and understand what the story implies, you know that you have had conferred upon you a very special privilege. You are no longer a guest. You are family.

Families that do not operate on the intimacy by inclusion paradigm tend to adopt an "us against them" stance. At the first threat of invasion from the outside they circle the wagons, join forces and fight fiercely against the marauder, be it a person, a situation or an institution. Families that value intimacy also band together in times of trouble, but the difference is that once the threat has been safely warded off, they do not continue fighting within. Families that thrive on drama and trauma, on the other hand, tend to turn against their own. Allegiances shift and sway depending on the climate, but there is almost always somebody on the outside looking in. Though a great deal of what looks like intimacy springs up among the various factions in families like these, it is not the kind that can be trusted. It is intimacy by exclusion, and it flourishes only as long as the fires of discontent are fueled. Not surprisingly, their stories rarely enter the realm of the sacred.

The saddest thing I learned in the course of the interviews for this book was how alienated too many people feel from their extended families. When they see them at all, it is from a sense of duty or a vague hope that maybe, somehow, a miracle will take place and next Christmas will be just like the one on *Family Matters*. But beneath all that deep regret and vague longing I also sensed an understanding that it really does not work that way. As much as we would like to believe that happy, healthy families pop full-blown out of Hallmark cards and TV sit-coms when December 25 rolls around, most of us know deep down that they do not. Happy families are built, experience by experience, story by story, ritual by ritual, throughout the seasons and years of our lives.

Most of the people I talked to who struggle with difficult pasts are working hard to keep history from repeating itself with their own children and are trying to mend what fences they can. To them goes my deepest respect and admiration. It is not easy to break ground without a blueprint or to build a sturdy house when there is no firm foundation, but they are trying, and for the most part are drawing sound diagrams. Because of their heroic efforts, their children will be spared the pain of having to build from the ground up when they in turn confront the challenge of raising children in the twenty-first century.

Happily, most of the families that invited me in for a glimpse of their story life take pride in a rich, vibrant, ever-growing tradition that has been passed along to them like a set of treasured china. There may be a few cracks, even a chip here and there, but for the most part they are as whole and happy as families get. Instead of aiming to be "perfect," they aim to be real, to love one another in good times and bad, and to add new stories every day to the story bag they have treasured for generations. Psychologist Mary Pipher promotes stories and rituals as a way for families to protect each other. I like that word *protect*, though pop psychology would probably frown and would label protection a form of codependency. I prefer, as Pipher does, to think of it as *inter*dependency.

The truth is that we need each other. When the evening news dishes up stories about parents abusing, neglecting and killing their own children, we need reassurance that there is still such a thing as safety. When we read newspaper headlines about African-American churches being senselessly burned to the ground and bombs exploding on planes and at the Olympic Games, we need to be able to turn to one another as an antidote to despair. And when we grind through the impersonal mechanizations of modern bureaucracy, we need to know that somebody has left the porch light on to welcome us home.

For some of us, myself included, the parameters of family have widened over the years to make room for what author Madeleine L'Engle calls "friends of the right hand." These are the few, special people who inch over the line that separates even very dear friends from family. To choose (or to be chosen) as family is a process that happens only rarely, and seldom quickly, for the simple reason that it requires participants to assume all the complicated, uncomfortable and downright wretched parts of family life along with the warm fuzzies that make us feel good. Those who cross the line are in for the long haul, which means that when they encounter a glitch, even a big one, they can be counted on to stick around and work it out, even when the path leading in the opposite direction looks infinitely more enticing. Because it is a major commitment, we can choose or be chosen only when we understand what a sacred, all-encompassing act it is to regard one another as family.

Not long after I began the research for this book, I was talking on the phone to Jessica, a friend who sometime over the last decade crept over the line and became family. In the middle of a discussion about our daughters, we somehow switched gears and launched into a story we must have told each other a hundred times. We each said the things we always say and laughed uproariously at the same points we always laugh at. Anyone overhearing us would almost certainly have thought it the first time we had ever rehashed the experience. But this time we caught ourselves in the act.

"Do you see what's happening here?" I asked her.

"Yep," she replied cheerfully, "we're bonding."

And so we were. As families do, we were trotting out a story unique to us and our relationship, a story that would cause any bystanders to shake their heads and wander away muttering about men in white coats. But because it reminds us that ours is an uncommon bond, this silly little story (which I refuse to disclose on the grounds that it is too embarrassing) will undoubtedly send us into the same delicious hysterics when we are eighty-five. We do not tell it because it is especially unique or amazing, or because it makes us look clever or heroic, but because it reminds us of a moment when we were swept away by pure, unbridled glee and nobody but us knew why.

Of all the many gifts family stories bring to your life, this strong, sheltering intimacy is its most precious legacy. In a sense, it is the shield that protects your family from the slings and arrows of the larger world. When the company downsizes, the scholarship does not materialize, the first love ends in heartbreak and the kids around the corner do not let you play, it is not the Power Rangers or the characters on *Chicago Hope* who listen to your grief, dry your tears and help you figure out what to do next. It is your family—the people who by birth, adoption or choice have agreed to open their hearts and doors to you whenever—day or night—you need a listening ear, a warm hug or a cup of hot tea.

Over the course of my research I collected so many examples of family stories' drawing us together that it would be impossible to tell them all, though I am tempted to try. In some ways I have saved the best for last because these stories, which illustrate the special intimacy of family, are the ones that filled me with the most hope. After more than a year of lurid newspaper headlines about family murders, I was more than ready for a happy ending. I also desperately needed to hear that as technology leaps ever onward, some families still care enough to occasionally unplug themselves from the electronic community to enjoy the community residing under their own roofs. Again, these stories are not amazing or extraordinary, and you probably know many that are much more compelling, but I offer them as small pearls—gifts from the deep.

Survival Stories

One type of story families tell with particular zest is the survival story. Whether they braved the forces of nature or of city hall, their delight in having prevailed together gleams like a newly minted silver dollar. Survival stories take many forms, but their common denominator is the fact that the entire family pulled together as a team, withstood pain, suffering, fear, disaster and so on, and emerged from the ordeal strong and whole. Families love to recount these escapades, not only to remind themselves how lucky they were to have walked safely through the fire but to affirm the sacredness of their interdependency. One of my favorite survival stories is told by Laura Oliver, a talented writer from Annapolis, Maryland, who shared with her children a night none of them will ever forget. As with most near-miss stories, this one recounts an experience they would rather not have had. But more importantly, it illustrates the way warm, close families manage to turn difficult situations into redemptive moments.

One evening when Laura was seven months pregnant and her husband was three thousand miles away on a business trip, a fierce August storm blew up late at night. Armed with an oil lamp and a book of matches, she felt no cause for alarm as she climbed the stairs to bed. Her two young children had been asleep for hours, and she felt sure that the lightening zigzagging across the dark sky would be deflected by the trees, most of which were taller than the house. Seconds later, a blinding bolt of electricity split the forty-eight-foot maple in the front yard, disrupting the power. The clock and the air conditioner went dead.

As the wind keened against the beat of driving rain and resounding claps of thunder, her eight-year-old daughter, Audra, appeared at her side in search of refuge. Groping in the dark, Laura pulled back the sheet on her bed. Audra climbed in and fell asleep at once, leaving her mother to toss and turn in the stuffy room. As the heat grew more and more stifling, Laura weighed her options. She could either risk opening the unscreened windows or stay awake all night. Telling herself that it would take only a short while for the rainswept air to bring the temperature down, she chose the latter and soon dozed off. Moments later she awoke with a sense of foreboding.

Even without seeing it, she knew that something dark, ominous and *alive* had joined them in the bedroom. Heart pounding, she grabbed her matches and lit the oil lamp. The flame caught and flickered just as an enormous black bat swooped inches from her daughter's head. Instinctively, Laura grabbed Audra's arm and lurched for the door, dragging her half-awake child behind her. But as the door closed behind them, her heart sank to her feet. In her haste to sequester the bat, she had left the oil lamp burning on the nightstand!

There was no choice but to go back and get it. Gingerly, she inched open the door and slipped inside the dimly lit room. All she had to do, she told herself bravely, was focus on the lamp and move quickly, and she would be safely back out in the hall again. Unfortunately, she had not counted on the bat's having company. Instead of one, there were now *three* bats circling in a frenzied dance overhead. Seizing the lamp, she bolted out the door and slammed it shut behind her.

What happened next sounds like a slapstick comedy, but only if you were not there and if you knew in advance that everything would eventually work out fine. To make a long story short, one of the bats escaped through the small space where the wooden door, which had swelled in the humidity, failed to make contact with the frame. Laura and both kids staggered downstairs as one clutching, grasping, trembling entity, barricaded themselves in the kitchen, and spent a disquieting night on the kitchen floor arrayed like an "intricate puzzle" on an assortment of sofa cushions and afghans. At one point, Laura called a twenty-four-hour exterminator who told her that the bats had most likely sailed in on an air current and would most likely depart the same way. For $120, he informed her, he would gladly come over in the morning and take a look.

At daybreak she declared a holiday from school and called a friend instead of the exterminator. Armed with a broom and a cardboard box, her friend searched the folds of draperies and clothes, and even looked behind picture frames, but the bats had departed just as stealthily as they had arrived. In an article for *Country Living* magazine she summed up her family's harrowing experience like this: "The children love to tell the bat story to visitors. They interrupt each other to embellish the details. Their eyes shine as they gleefully recount the invasion and our retreat, the delicious danger. They are veterans with a war story they will tell for years to come. They don't remember we were afraid. They only recall we were comrades in arms, who served each other loyally, in the darkness of the night."[1]

This story enchanted me as soon as I heard it. Aside from being vivid and compelling, it recounts a rare and wondrous event. I am not referring to the bat invasion, though I think (and hope) that it is an uncommon event. What pleases me is the fact that for one brief moment in time the division between parent and child blurred. As adults, we bear the responsibility of protecting and sheltering our kids. And that, of course, is the way it should be. But the act of comforting and being comforted by their mother on a dark and stormy night gave Laura's children a rare glimpse into the meaning of interdependency, the very essence of intimacy. No wonder they love to recount the story to anyone who will listen!

Another survival story that delights me is one told by Diana Budney, the teacher from Lodi, Ohio. As a little girl growing up in the 1960s, she dearly loved the old TV soap opera *Dark Shadows,* even though it never failed to kick her already hyperactive imagination into overdrive. Knowing that she would be banned from watching if her mother ever found out the extent of her fear, she always feigned nonchalance whenever anyone asked her about it. One weekend the family went to West Virginia to visit her grandmother, who lived in an old restored house with twenty-eight-inch thick walls. It had been used at various times in the past as both a surgical hospital and a jail and was located not far from the railroad tracks.

The first night of their stay Diana woke up just before daybreak and had to go to the bathroom. Because the house was not plumbed upstairs, Diana had to make a terrifying trip down the creaky steps to the bathroom off the kitchen. Slowly and carefully, every nerve-ending buzzing, she crept down in the dark, trying hard not to think about *Dark Shadows.* At the bottom of the stairs she inched her way safely past the front parlor and down the hall to the kitchen. Only a few more steps to go, she told herself, and she would be . . .

Suddenly the back door sprang open. A man swathed head to toe in a dark cape stood silhouetted in the doorway, his arms piled high with something dark and menacing. Diana knew with sick certainty who it was—Barnabas Collins, the vampire from *Dark Shadows!* She passed out cold on the kitchen floor.

When she came to, her favorite uncle was crouching over her, his face filled with concern. He had driven by on his way to work and had decided to stop at his mother's house, bring in some wood, and get the fires lit for morning. To keep warm he had wrapped himself in an old blanket. Diana tearfully told him what had happened and begged him not to humiliate her by spilling the story to the rest of the family. Although an inveterate storyteller who could wring a laugh out of picking up the mail, he agreed to pass up the chance to tell a whopping tale.

Not long ago, Diana learned that her beloved Uncle Jim was dying of black lung disease. As the family gathered at his bedside to say goodby, he leaned over to Diana. "I never did tell, " he told her.

"Never did tell what?" the aunts, uncles and cousins demanded.

Diana knew at once what he meant. Laughing, she finally gave him the green light to tell the tale they had shared for more than two decades. When he wrapped it up, the family was astounded that their best yarn-spinner had managed to stifle such a juicy story. Only Diana was unsurprised. "I knew he'd never break my heart," she says simply. Diana's is a survival story with a twist. She survived a terrible fright but learned a powerful lesson about the meaning of trust in the process.

An interesting variation of the survival tale is the rescue story. Stories about rescuing a loved one from danger, disaster or their own foolhardiness are not about weathering hard times as much as they are about the moment of decision when we have the choice between wringing our hands in despair and doing something heroic. Most of the rescue stories I heard centered on saving family members from physical harm, but there is one that was so unique and intimate it haunted me throughout the writing of this book.

I met my friend Linda about seven years ago when she turned up in my office seeking a job as a companion to the elderly residents at the nursing home where I worked. The minute she sat down across from my desk, I knew I had discovered pure gold. It is not often that such a bright, articulate, attractive, warm and funny woman seeks a job that extracts an enormous commitment and pays most of its dividends in hugs instead of dollars. Although we have both gone our separate career paths since then, Linda remains a link to the nursing home and one of the most difficult periods of my life.

Almost from the beginning of our relationship I knew that she was a Christian. It is not something she announces or belabors. But you cannot help but notice it in her joyful, fun-loving, compassionate view of the world. It pained her that her father, with whom she shared an uncommonly close and loving relationship, considered himself an agnostic. Although they had debated the existence of God for years, she had never succeeded in convincing him to change his mind. Even after he contracted cancer and knew he was dying, spiritual issues seemed to hold no appeal.

Unexpectedly, a pivotal story for Linda and her family was written at the hospital where she and her mother were taking turns caring for her father around the clock in his final days. It was brutally hot that afternoon, his fever had spiked, and the hospital's air conditioning labored under the intense heat. To give him some relief, Linda filled a pan with cool water for the cloth she put on his forehead and set it on the bedside table next to her. By this time her dad was unable to speak but was still cognizant of what was going on around him. As Linda submerged the cloth in the water for the umpteenth time, she was suddenly seized by something more urgent than an idea or even an overwhelming desire.

Slowly, deliberately, she set the cloth down, dipped her hand in the water and sprinkled her father's forehead with the cool water.

"I baptize you in the name of the Father, the Son and the Holy Spirit," she said quietly.

He met her eyes and smiled.

Intimate Miracles

Of course it is not only stories of near misses, shared confidences and inspired rescues that bring families together. Sometimes intimacy occurs when a forgotten anecdote resurfaces and cuts a wide swath through the thick undergrowth of pain and misunderstanding, making room for new life to begin. Dylan, a young man in his thirties, discovered how a painful past and an awkward present can be healed and transformed by the simplest of stories.

Too often we tend to take family stories at face value, thereby failing to understand that beneath their simplicity lies an awesome and creative power.

Several years ago on Thanksgiving Day, sixteen members of Dylan's extended family, plus their children, converged at his sister Phoebe's house for a traditional turkey dinner with all the trimmings. They represented six family groups, several of whom had not spoken for several years due to a business deal that went sour and caused serious losses for two of them. Everyone had come at Phoebe's request, knowing how much she longed for a reconciliation. But few held out much hope for it. The family had gained two new in-laws since the falling-out, whom some of those present had never met. To say that the conversation in Phoebe's living room that day was stilted would be like saying that a roomful of finger-painting preschoolers is "a little messy." All sixteen adults held their collective breath waiting for the oven timer to buzz them into dinner so they could at least discuss the merits of sage versus chestnut dressing rather than stare at the carpet and make inane comments about the weather.

Desperate to break the ice, Dylan, a gregarious natural talker, finally said the first thing that popped into his head. "Hey, guess who I saw the other day—Mrs. Rhimer. Remember her? She must be at least ninety."

"I'll say I remember her!" his brother Evan answered eagerly. "I haven't sung a note since I got out of her sixth-grade music class."

"That's true," Evan's wife, Sara, chimed in. "Even at church he just mouths the words."

"Well, I never sang a note the whole time I was *in* her class," one of the new in-laws added. "I was a crow, and crows weren't aloud to sing, remember?"

"Yeah, they had to lip-sync!" Dylan agreed. "I was a crow too!"

Cries of "So was I!" and "Me too!" rang out from all corners of the room. The "crows" (all guys, ranging in age from thirty to fifty-eight) began swapping stories of their mutual humiliation. It seems that Mrs. Rhimer had made everyone in the class sing a solo during the first week of school so she could assess the vocal ability of her new charges. Those with the best voices were labeled the bluebirds and got to stand in front. The mediocre singers, otherwise known as the robins, held up the center section, while the crows were relegated to the back row where they had to lip-sync their way through "She'll Be Comin' Round the Mountain."

Hearing the laughter from the living room, Phoebe left her dinner preparations to stand in the doorway. "Well," she informed the group with mock smugness, "I'll have you know that it was up to *me* to salvage the reputation of this family. I may not have made it to bluebird, but at least I made robinhood."

"Robin Hood!" one of the children yelled, pretending to fire an imaginary bow and arrow. The room exploded in laughter that pealed like bells ringing out the old grievances and welcoming in a new spirit of forgiveness and hope.

Such a small story, such a miracle of intimacy.

There is one other story I want to tell about the miracle of intimacy, a story that is not small. I learned of it a few days ago when I was having coffee with my friend Diane Walker, with whom I shared the persistent feeling that something was still missing, even though I had heard literally hundreds of wonderful stories during my interviews for this book. "I don't know what it is," I confided. "It's like there's something left undone, but I don't know where I'm supposed to look to find it. I've talked to so many people already. I don't know who else I should be talking to."

For a short while we weighed my dilemma. Then she told me several stories of her own that left me limp with laughter. We had just decided to head for home when suddenly her eyes widened. "Oh, I almost forgot to tell you! " she cried. "Did you see the Tess story in the paper the other day? I thought of you when I read it."

Though I have read Noreen Anderson's column, *Et Cetera,* in the *Medina County Gazette* for years, I had somehow overlooked the one in question, so Diane was obliged to recap it. Before she had even finished filling me in on the details, I knew I had to call the writer. I was not sure that it was my "missing story," but I was intrigued enough to find out more. Several days later, as I listened to Noreen tell me the story herself, I knew that it was what I had been looking for. Hearing Noreen tell it in her own words, with her own awe still skimming its surface, raised goosebumps on my skin and reminded me that nothing equals the immediacy of a story told by the one who lived it. It reminded me that blessings arrive daily from heaven. We just need to claim them. I needed a special story, and one had arrived for me just in the nick of time.

Five years ago, when she was forty-five, Noreen was diagnosed with breast cancer. As the mother of ten children, the youngest of whom was only five at the time, she was wrenched by the thought that she might not live to see them all grow up. That night, as she sat on the porch weeping for all she stood to lose, she suddenly realized that she might miss the joy of grandchildren too. As a child who had grown up longing for a grandmother, she had always been eager to assume that role someday. But now it looked like it might never happen, all because of a few cells run amok.

In the following days Noreen's doctors presented her with a single ray of hope—an extremely potent and grueling course of chemotherapy. It would make her deathly ill and cause her hair to fall out, and there were no guarantees of success. But it was the best treatment medical science had to offer. She accepted it gratefully and began a horrific journey toward wellness. Not long after the treatment began, however, she experienced a dream so vivid it did not seem like a dream at all.

During this night vision Noreen was walking barefoot along the New England coastline, hand in hand with a tall, slender girl with long brown hair. The surf lapped gently at their feet and soaked the bottoms of their long, full skirts, but they did not mind. They were free spirits enjoying the sublime pleasure of being alive and being together on a glorious blue and gold Cape Cod day. Somehow she sensed that she was seventy and the girl was twenty. She also sensed that the girl was her granddaughter and that her name was Tess. So vivid and detailed was this vision that even now she can see clearly the curtains of a weathered gray beach house blowing in the breeze, hear the pounding of the surf, and feel what it was like to be there, even though she has never visited Cape Cod or New England. For some reason she told no one about the dream. It was enough to quietly hold fast to the image, thank God the gift of it and draw on its strength during the difficult months that followed.

Noreen is now fifty and cancer-free. Not long ago, her married daughter announced that a new baby will be born later this year—a girl. It did not take Noreen long to calculate that when she is seventy, the baby will be twenty. Could it be, she wondered, that this is would be the child she dreamed of? Afraid to even hold the thought in her mind, much less her heart, she said nothing until her daughter added the clincher—the baby's name will be Tess.[2]

Present and future, sickness and health, dreams and reality, youth and old age, grandmothers and granddaughters—like fine silk threads intertwined on the loom of the Master Weaver, they come together to create a story that is intimate enough to bind three generations and universal enough to speak to the needs of a million hearts. Before she told it to me, my friend Diane had sent a copy of the Tess story to a neighbor who had just been diagnosed with breast cancer. When it reached her, she was lying in the intensive care unit of a major metropolitan hospital, but she was able to read it and take hope. This hope is the reason we must share our family stories.

Ebb and Flow

Though it seems impossible, a year has passed since I first started talking to people about their family stories. I must confess that I came to the task with a certain smugness. From early childhood I had known that the act of using words to breathe life into something that had already happened was a magical and mysterious thing. All of my life I have been a collector of stories—stories told to me, stories read, stories overheard, snippets of stories that drifted past me in a crowd like wisps of smoke. But all of it was only an overture to the symphony of stories that awaited me as I set about the task of asking people to share with me the memories of their lives.

Several hundred stories and almost fifteen hundred storytelling hours later, I am neither sated with stories nor smug about them. I am awed, humbled and *thrilled* to have witnessed their power to bind, heal, protect and bless our families. Every story I heard, whether it appears in this book or not, taught me something new and shaped my understanding of the unmistakable link between storytelling and the love and creativity of God. Like life, family stories are forever fluid. When one ends, a new one rushes in to take its place. So it seems fitting that as my mind focused on ebb and flow, my own family should see one story come to an end and a fresh new one begin in its place.

On July 20, 1996, our daughter Moira and her boyfriend of three years, Brian Watson, announced their engagement. It was Brian's mother's birthday, and his family had traveled three hours from Michigan to be our guests for the weekend. Just as we were sitting down to Saturday-night dinner, Moira and Brian stood up and stunned us all with their announcement. When the laughter, tears and hugs subsided, I gazed around the table at the shining faces we are just beginning to know and felt deeply, deeply blessed. It seems especially fitting to conclude this book where it began—in the Wedgwood-blue-and-white dining room where the cast of characters spilling out into the foyer and cramming the kitchen grows wondrously larger.

The Ekoi people of Nigeria say that a long time ago stories were like story children woven from whatever was "in the house of the world." The storyteller was the guardian of the story children and, as such, had four responsibilities: to see that the story child had a beautiful gown all her own, distinct from, yet connected to, the gowns of all the other story children; to allow the story child to be inspired by all that is hidden; to see that the story child speaks her own truth; and to allow her to run free, to have her own voice.[3]

As you encounter the realities of ebb and flow in your own life, remember it, for sacred stories are indeed like children. They grow and change, bring about endings and beginnings, make you laugh and weep and sometimes do both simultaneously. If you root them deep in the soil of the family circle, they grow and flourish and produce much fruit. But you cannot keep them there forever. They are born to speak their own truth, to run free and to have their own voice. And their truth can change the world.

Tips for Family Storytelling

1. Maintain close physical proximity to your audience. Small children love to climb up on your lap or snuggle into a big chair for storytelling. (Even big kids like the latter from time to time!) For a large group, try a circle arrangement. The presence of the storyteller is a key element in the overall experience.

2. Live your story! Enjoy the act of telling it. Don't be afraid to use sound effects, voice changes, dialogue, hand gestures, puppets and props.

3. Always have a very specific setting for your story—Grandma's kitchen, the back room of Uncle Don's clock shop and so on.

4. Draw your audience into the action by using as many sensory details as possible. Help your listener see, hear, smell, feel and taste it.

5. Develop special story phrases that help set the mood. Openers such as "Once upon a time" or "Long, long ago, before you were even born" heighten the sense of anticipation.

6. For more formal storytelling events, set the mood by lighting a special candle, ringing a bell or passing a "story stone"—any ritualistic activity that tells the audience that it is time to move from "real time" to "story time."

7. When telling stories to small children, build in repetition and allow them to conarrate. A single phrase or a few nonsense syllables capture their attention and engage them in the action. Small children love stories about themselves.

8. Resist the urge to tack on a moral. It is okay to ask, "What did you think about that?" But don't say, "See why you should always . . ." or "And that's how so-and-so learned . . ."

9. Be careful not to tell stories that have the potential to embarrass, frighten or upset any member of the family, even if that person is not present. Don't use storytelling to shame or manipulate anyone.

10. Encourage children to tell their own stories by asking questions and giving them your full attention when they speak.

11. Don't use story time to correct your children's grammar, syntax or tense. Resist the urge to take their story away from them by arranging the events in a more logical sequence. They will learn volumes about language by repeated exposure to the process and by being allowed to tell their own stories in their own words.

12. Expose kids to a wide variety of story forms and subjects. Allow them equal latitude even when they want to recount the plot of a movie or TV show. Very often kids tell these stories because they matter to them.

13. Allow the audience to interact with the storyteller! Don't squelch playful bantering, questions or challenges. Encourage creativity.

14. Research has shown that stories help reduce stress, even when a child is sick or in pain. Give children the idea that by sitting quietly and listening they will begin to feel better.

15. Don't worry about whether or not you have your kids' full attention. They take in a great deal more than they appear to even when they are doing something else.

16. Allow certain stories to be "owned" by certain members of the family. If Aunt Molly loves the story about the time she accidentally made a tuna casserole with cat food tuna, let *her* be the one to tell it.

Storytelling Resources

Storytelling Organizations

International Order of E.A.R.S., 12019 Donahue Ave., Louisville, KY 40243. Lee Pennington, director. Tel. (502) 245-0643. Founded 1983. Membership: 1,000. Regional groups: 1. Dues: $15 single, $25 family. Promotes interest in storytelling, conducts storytelling performances and operates the Storytelling Resource Center, consisting of books and two thousand cataloged stories on video and audiotape.

National Association of Black Storytellers, P.O. Box 67722, Baltimore, MD 21215. Founded 1984. Membership: 400. State groups: 3. Dues: $20 individual, $10 senior, $5 youth. Purpose is to promote the African oral tradition and to work to reissue out-of-print story collections. Publishes newsletter and annual handbook.

National Storytelling Association, P.O. Box 309, Jonesborough, TN 37659. Tel. (424) 753-2171. Founded 1975. Membership: 7,000. Dues: $40 annually; includes subscription to bimonthly *Storytelling Magazine.* Hosts National Storytelling Festival in Jonesborough on the first full weekend in October. Also hosts annual conference.

National Story League. Contact Alic Brynteson, 901 Hyak Place, Fox Island, WA 98333. Tel. (206) 549-2495. Founded 1903. Membership: 15,000. Regional groups: 3. State groups: 45. Local groups: 250. Members volunteer to tell and record stories in places like schools, churches, nursing homes, hospitals. Operates National Story Junior League. Conducts seminars and writing workhops.

Network of Biblical Storytellers. Contact Mary Cooper, coordinator, Union Theological Seminary, 1810 Harvard Blvd., Dayton, OH 45406. Tel. (800)-355-NOBS. Founded 1978. Membership: 325 dues paying, 600 mailing list. Dues: $30 annually; includes quarterly newsletter and annual journal. Group works to foster the telling of biblical stories in the electronic age. Sponsors annual summer conference and storytelling festival.

Books

Greene, Bob, and D. G. Fulford. *To Our Children's Children: Preserving Family Histories for Generations to Come.* New York: Doubleday, 1993. Great resource for story prompts, especially for elder stories.

Polking, Kirk. *Writing Family Histories and Memoirs.* Cincinnati: Betterway Books. Easy-to-follow instructions for getting ideas, researching, interviewing and writing family stories for historical preservation.

Games

Atlas Games, P.O. Box 131233, Roseville, MN 551113. Tel. (612) 638-0098. Manufacturer of Once upon a Time interactive storytelling card game. Available in toy and book stores, $15.95, or direct from manufacturer. Add $3 postage and handling. ISBN 1-887801-06-6.

Internet

There are over nine hundred sites pertaining to storytelling and related topics. My favorite is http://users.aol.com/storypage. Jim Maroon offers a comprehensive listing of storytelling organizations state by state, as well as resources for storytellers. There is even a chat room if you have a yen to talk to other storytellers.

Catalogs

Yellow Moon Press, P.O. Box 1316, Dept. 38, Cambridge, MA 02238. Tel. (800) 497-4385. A comprehensive collection of storytelling materials including both how-to manuals and story collections on tape and in books. Free catalog.

Credence Cassettes, 115 E. Armour Blvd., Kansas City, MO 64111-1203. Tel. (816) 531-0530. Producer of wide range of audiotapes, primarily on religious topics, many of which apply to storytelling.

Education

Disney Institute, Lake Buena Vista, FL. Tel. (407) 827-4800. Opened February 9, 1996. Guests may select story arts track, one of nine concepts featured in the institute's programming. Study focuses on Disney story, world of storytelling and youth. The National Storytelling Association was consulted on early stages of program planning.

East Tennessee State University, School of Graduate Studies, P.O. Box 70720, Johnson City, TN 37614-0720. Tel. (423) 929-6146. Offers master's degree in storytelling.

Emerson College School of Storytelling, Registration Secretary, Forest Row, East Sussex, RH 185JX, England. Tel. (01342) 822238, or fax (01342) 826055. Offers a thirteen-week course for teachers, storytellers, therapists, parents and actors. Also conducts annual International Storytelling Symposium.

Kanuga Conferences, Postal Drawer 250, Hendersonville, NC 28793. Tel. (704) 692-9136. An Episcopal conference center located on fourteen hundred acres in the Blue Ridge Mountains. Meals, accommodations, children's and youth programs. Offers various summer conferences, usually one per year on storytelling with emphasis on ministry.

Sacred Heart University, Fairfield, CT. Offers master's degree program in storytelling; weekends and summers. Contact Wendy Nowlan, The Learning Collaborative, 701 North St., Milford, CT 06460. Tel. (203) 878-5939 or fax 203-874-8070.

The School of Sacred Storytelling, 18934 Rolling Road, Hagerstown, MD 21742. Tel. (301) 791-9153 or (800) 277-7035; http://www.storyfest.com. Founded in 1979 by Robert B. Wilhelm. Sponsors storytelling concerts, festivals and seminars throughout the United States and Canada, as well as storytelling trips to Ireland, Scotland, Cornwall, Wales, Italy, Bermuda and the South Pacific. Also offers a storytelling apprenticeship program for ministers, teachers, counselors, health-care providers and church leaders. Each year, eight new apprentices enter the three-summer program to learn to become master storytellers.

Storytellers School of Toronto, 791 St. Clair Ave. W., 2nd Floor, Toronto, Ont. M6C1B7. Tel. (416) 656-2445. Offers both weekend and summer workshops covering a wide variety of subjects relating to the fine art of storytelling. 1997 topics include telling stories to children, humor, women's stories, biblical storytelling and the use of the voice, as well as basics for beginners.

Survivors of the Shoah Visual History Foundation, P.O. Box 3168, Los Angeles, CA 90078-3168. Tel. (800) 661-2092. Hours: Mon.-Fri. 9:30 a.m.—5:00 p.m. (Pacific). Founded by director Steven Spielberg to provide more than 100,000 hours of Holocaust survivor testimony for education and historical preservation.

Washington Storytellers Theatre, P.O. Box 5564, Washington, D.C. 20016. Tel. (202) 291-2170. Offers a wide range of storytelling workshops and concerts by the country's leading storytellers, including Don Davis.

Notes

Chapter 1: Outpowering the Power Rangers

[1]The quote attributed to author James Carroll can be found in Madeleine L'Engle's book *The Rock That Is Higher* (Wheaton, Ill.: Harold Shaw, 1993). Carroll is the author of numerous works of fiction and nonfiction that explore the Irish Catholic family experience. His fiction, published by Little, Brown (Boston), includes *Family Trade* (1982), *Fault Lines* (1980) and *Mortal Friends* (1978). His most recent work is the nonfiction narrative *An American Requiem: God, My Father and the War That Came Between Us* (Boston: Houghton Mifflin, 1996).

[2]For color photos and the complete history of Cochiti storyteller figurines, see David L. Arnold, "Pueblo Pottery, 2000 Years of Artistry," *National Geographic*, November 1982, p. 599.

[3]The quotes attributed to storyteller Don Davis derived from a telephone interview conducted by the author in January 1993. Davis is the author of *Telling Your Own Stories: For Family and Classroom Storytelling, Public Speaking and Personal Journaling* (Little Rock, Ark.: August House, 1993).

[4]For further information on the effect of Internet surfing on the academic performance of college students, see Rene Sanchez, "Hooked Online and Sinking: Cybersurfing Crowds Out College Work," *The Washington Post*, May 22, 1996.

[5]For a complete and entertaining history of the National Storytelling Association and the National Storytelling Festival and their impact on the small town of Jonesborough, Tennessee, see editor Jimmy Neil Smith's foreword to the book *Homespun: Tales from America's Favorite Storytellers* (New York: Crown, 1988).

[6]The quote attributed to George Gerbner, dean emeritus of the University of Pennsylvania's Annenberg School of Communications, can be found in *Current Biography Yearbook*, edited by Charles Moritz (New York: H. W. Wilson, 1983). For an in-depth look at Gerbner's theories on the relationship of violent media representations and marketing strategy see Nancy McCray, *The Killing Screens:*

Media and the Culture of Violence (Northampton, Mass.: Media Education Foundation, 1994).

[7]For further commentary on the diminishing quality of television and its effect on children, see David Denby, "Buried Alive: Our Children and the Avalanche of Crud," *The New Yorker,* July 15, 1996, pp. 48-58.

[8]Commentary on the importance of family stories for historical preservation and personal growth can be found in Madeleine L'Engle's "Tell Me a Story," *Victoria,* April 1995, pp. 32-33. L'Engle served as writer in residence for the magazine in 1995. For a commentary on the increasing use of narrative in fiction, law and science, see Bill Buford, "The Seductions of Storytelling: Why Is Narrative Suddenly So Popular?" *The New Yorker,* June 24/July 1, 1996, pp. 11-12.

Chapter 2: Coming Back to the Fire

[1]While Alex Haley's landmark *Roots* (Garden City, N.Y.: Doubleday, 1976) did much to heighten interest in genealogy generally, its value lies in its emotionally compelling presentation of how cultural identity is shaped and nurtured through the power of story. It influenced me deeply twenty years ago—revisiting it in the context of my premise for this book served only to strengthen my convictions.

[2]The collective body of work by Sam Keen likewise influenced my thoughts regarding storytelling and identity. See especially *Telling Your Story* (New York: Sound Horizons, 1991) and *Telling Your Story: A Guide to Who You Are and What You Can Be,* with Ann Valley Fox (Garden City, N.Y.: Doubleday, 1973). I also credit the work of Matthew Fox in shaping my understanding of cultural and societal influences on the formation of identity.

[3]For a first-person account of the American missionary experience in India during the nineteenth century from the perspective of a Presbyterian missionary family from Pennsylvania, see Barbara Tull, *Affectionately, Rachel: Letters from India, 1860-1884* (Kent, Ohio: Kent State University Press, 1992).

[4]The quote attributed to Alexis de Tocqueville can be found in Elizabeth Stone's *Black Sheep and Kissing Cousins: How Our Family Stories Shape Us* (New York: Times Books, 1988), which also deepened my understanding of why families exaggerate their collective talents and seek out stories of illustrious ancestors.

Chapter 3: Building Cathedrals

[1]For further information on the relationship between storytelling and children's values, see Charles A. Smith, *From Wonder to Wisdom: Using Stories to Help Children Grow* (New York: New American Library, 1989), and Norma Livo and Sandra A. Reitz, *Storytelling: Process and Practice* (Littleton, Colo.: Libraries Unlimited, 1986).

[2]The broadcast concerning children's attitudes toward moral values aired on *Prime*

Time Live (ABC) with Diane Sawyer, February 14, 1996.

[3]For the quote attributed to Ernest Becker and a deeper look at the concept of heroes, see Rollo May, *The Cry for Myth* (New York: W. W. Norton, 1991).

Chapter 4: Bandaging the Soul

[1]The quote attributed to Elie Wiesel can be found in the audiotape *Sacred Storytelling*, by Midge Miles (Kansas City, Mo.: Credence Cassettes, 1993). Wiesel's memoir *All Rivers Run to the Sea* (New York: Alfred A. Knopf, 1995) offers the complete story of his internment in the concentration camps of Nazi Germany and how this shaped his life as an author, educator and Nobel Prize winner.

[2]The information on Survivors of the Shoah appeared in Harvey Solomon's "Never Forget: Spielberg Gives Survivors Forum to Tell Chilling Stories of the Holocaust," *Medina County Gazette*, December 27, 1995, p. 10.

[3]The reference to the study by Barbara H. Fiese of Syracuse University about the types of stories parents tell based on gender appeared in Joyce Brothers's column "Your Questions Answered: How Childhood Stories Connect Us," *Good Housekeeping*, August 1996, p. 28.

[4]For an in-depth look at how the modality a storyteller employs influences audience response, see Sam Keen's audiotape *The Power of Stories: Illuminating Your Life's Meaning Through Stories* (Boulder, Colo.: Sounds True Audiotapes, 1992).

[5]For both the image of the story bag and further information on storytelling during times of transition, see Alida Gersie, *Earthtales: Storytelling in Times of Change* (London: Merlin, 1992).

Chapter 5: Finding God at the Fireside

[1]The quote and thoughts attributed to Tom Driver can be found in his book *Patterns of Grace: Human Experience as the Word of God* (San Francisco: Harper & Row, 1977). A student of theologian Paul Tillich, Driver wrote that the task of the theologian, like that of the actor, is to "go beyond split consciousness to find, in a lifetime of work, purity of heart beneath one's mask." His work especially influenced my thoughts on the subject of storytelling and religious ritual.

[2]Likewise, I attribute a deeper understanding of the correlation between storytelling and spirituality to Andrew M. Greeley, *Religion as Poetry* (New Brunswick, N.J.: Transaction, 1995), and Cindy Guthrie, "Telling Stories That Tell Truths," *Christian Ministry*, January/February 1996, pp. 17-19.

[3]For the source of my inspiration on the topic of stories and embellishment, see Alida Gersie and Nancy King, *Storymaking in Education and Therapy* (London: Jessica Kingsley; Stockholm: Stockholm Institute of Education Press, 1990).

[4]The definition of myth attributed to Robert Johnson can be found in Robin Moore's book *Awakening the Hidden Storyteller: How to Build a Storytelling Tradition in*

Your Family (Boston: Shambhala, 1991).

[5]For my understanding of the relationship between myth and storytelling, I am especially grateful to the collective work of Sam Keen and to Rollo May, *The Cry for Myth* (New York: W. W. Norton, 1991).

[6]The quote about storytelling and prayer attributed to Elizabeth Cody Newenhuyse derives from a personal interview conducted by the author. Newenhuyse is a popular writer on Christian topics. One of her recent books is *God, I Know You're in Here Somewhere: Finding God in the Clutter of Life* (Minneapolis: Bethany House, 1996).

[7]The lines attributed to Edna St. Vincent Millay are taken from the poem "God's World" (1917).

[8]The reference to Bill Martin, author and editor of the Sounds of Language reading series, can be found in the National Storytelling Association's book *Tales as Tools: The Power of Story in The Classroom* (Jonesborough, Tenn.: National Storytelling Association, 1994).

[10]For the liturgy of the Eucharist see Rite II, The Book of Common Prayer, 1979 edition.

Chapter 6: Stopping at the Troll Bridge

[1]For further information on storytelling as it relates to children, see Susan Engel, *The Stories Children Tell: Making Sense of the Narratives of Childhood* (New York: W. H. Freeman, 1995); Jane M. Healy, *How to Have Intelligent and Creative Conversations with Your Kids* (New York: Doubleday, 1996); and Ann M. Trousdale, Sue A. Woestehoff and Marni Schwartz, *Give a Listen: Stories of Storytelling in School* (Urbana, Ill.: National Council of Teachers of English, 1994).

[2]For information on the children of Bosnia and the SOS Kinderdorf Center, see Alexandar S. Dragicevic, "War Orphans Tell Tales to Rebuild Lives," *The Plain Dealer,* June 2, 1996, p. 14A.

[3]I was also deeply influenced by the work of Jose Hobday, a Roman Catholic nun, who shares the stories of her childhood on the audiotape *The Spiritual Power of Storytelling* (Kansas City, Mo.: Credence Cassettes, 1980).

Chapter 7: Passing on the Wisdom

[1]The story told by Garson Kanin can be found in his book *It Takes a Long Time to Become Young: An Entertainment in the Form of a Declaration of War Against the Mindless Youth Culture That Has Our Time in Its Grip* (New York: Doubleday, 1978). I have paraphrased it here.

[2]The Foxfire books, *Foxfire 1* through *Foxfire 10,* were published by Anchor/ Doubleday (New York) from 1976 to 1993.

[3]For further information on collecting elder stories, see Robert U. Alceret, *Family Tales, Family Wisdom: How to Gather the Stories of a Lifetime and Share Them with Your Family* (New York: William Morrow, 1991).

Chapter 8: Unraveling the Yarns

[1]Karen Cushman's Newbery Honor novel *Catherine, Called Birdy* was published in 1994 by Clarion (New York).

[2]For further information about the work of Elisabeth Kübler-Ross in the field of death and dying, see Sutor Davis, "Lessons for the Living in Death and Dying: An Interview with Elisabeth Kübler-Ross," *National Catholic Reporter,* April 20, 1973, p. 11.

[3]The quote attributed to Hildegard of Bingen (1098-1179) can be found in the preface to Matthew Fox's book *Whee! We, Wee All the Way Home: A Guide to Sensual Prophetic Spirituality* (Santa Fe, N.M.: Bear, 1981), p. 15.

[4]The children's books referred to in the text include *Moving Molly* by Shirley Hughes (New York: Lothrop, Lee and Shepard, 1988) and *Goodnight Moon* by Margaret Wise Brown (New York: Harper & Row, 1947). Beverly Cleary's Beezus and Ramona books span three decades, beginning with *Henry and Beezus* (New York: William Morrow, 1952) and ending with *Ramona Forever* (New York: William Morrow, 1984). The Betsy-Tacy books were written during the 1940s by Maude Hart Lovelace and published by Crowell Harper, New York. They include *Betsy and Tacy* (1940), *Betsy, Tacy and Tib* (1941), *Heavens to Betsy* (1945) and *Betsy in Spite of Herself* (1946).

[5]Walter Wangerin, *The Book of God: The Bible as a Novel* (Grand Rapids, Mich: Zondervan, 1996); Marjorie Holmes, *Two from Galilee* (Old Tappan, N.J.: Revell, 1972).

Chapter 9: Marking the Moments

[1]For the complete text of the Te Deum Laudamus, see Morning Prayer, Rite I, in The Book of Common Prayer, 1979 edition, pp. 52-53.

[2]Carl A. Hammerschlag, *The Theft of the Spirit: A Journey to Spiritual Healing with Native Americans* (New York: Simon & Schuster, 1993), p. 26.

[3]For further information about the role of storytelling and ritual, see Robert Fulghum, *From Beginning to End: The Rituals of Our Lives* (New York: Villard, 1995).

[4]Mary Pipher, *The Shelter of Each Other: Rebuilding Our Families* (New York: G. P. Putnam, 1996).

Chapter 10: Completing the Circle

[1]For the entire bat story, see Laura Oliver, "Comrades in Arms," *Country Living,* August 1995, p. 34.

[2]For the Tess story, see Noreen Anderson, "Life Is a Gamble—and the Rewards Are Infinite," *Medina County Gazette,* July 2, 1996, Lifestyle sec., p. C2.

[3]For the Ekoi people's philosophy of the ultimate goal of stories, see Alida Gersie, *Storytelling in Bereavement* (London: Jessica Kingsley, 1991).

Bibliography

Alceret, Robert U. *Family Tales, Family Wisdom: How to Gather the Stories of a Lifetime and Share Them with Your Family.* New York: William Morrow, 1991.

Buford, Bill. "The Seductions of Storytelling: Why Is Narrative Suddenly So Popular?" *The New Yorker,* June 24/July 1, 1996, pp. 11-12.

Carney, Jim. "Revival in the Art of Storytelling." *Akron Beacon Journal,* November 2, 1989, pp. E1-2.

Davis, Don. *Telling Your Own Stories.* Little Rock, Ark.: August House, 1993.

Davis, Sutor. "Lessons for the Living in Death and Dying: An Interview with Elisabeth Kübler-Ross." *National Catholic Reporter,* April 20, 1973, p. 11.

Denby, David. "Buried Alive: Our Children and the Avalanche of Crud." *The New Yorker,* July 15, 1996, pp. 48-58.

Driver, Tom F. *Patterns of Grace: Human Experience as the Word of God.* San Francisco: Harper & Row, 1977.

Engel, Susan. *The Stories Children Tell: Making Sense of the Narratives of Childhood.* New York: W. H. Freeman, 1995.

Feldman, Christina, and Jack Kornfield, eds. *Stories of the Spirit, Stories of the Heart: Parables of the Spiritual Path from Around the World.* San Francisco: Harper & Row, 1991.

Fox, Mathew. *Whee! We, Wee All the Way Home.* Santa Fe, N.M.: Bear, 1981.

Fulghum, Robert. *From Beginning to End: The Rituals of Our Lives.* New York: Villard Books, 1995.

George-Warren, Holly. "All in the Family." *Storytelling Magazine,* Winter 1992, pp. 16-17

Gersie, Alida. *Earthtales: Storytelling in Times of Change.* London: Merlin Press, 1992.
———. *Storytelling in Bereavement.* London: Jessica Kingsley, 1991.

Gersie, Alida, and Nancy King. *Storymaking in Education and Therapy.* London: Jessica Kingsley; Stockholm: Stockholm Institute of Education Press, 1990.

Greeley, Andrew M. *Religion as Poetry.* New Brunswick/London: Transaction Publishers, 1995.

Gutherie, Cindy. "Telling Stories That Tell Truths." *Christian Ministry,* January/February, 1996, pp. 17-19.

Healy, Jane M. *How to Have Intelligent and Creative Conversations with Your Kids.* New York: Doubleday, 1996.

Hobday, Jose. *The Spiritual Power of Storytelling.* Kansas City, Mo.: Credence Cassettes,1980.

Keen, Sam. *The Power of Stories: Illuminating Your Life's Meaning Through Stories.* Boulder, Colo.: Sounds True Audiotapes, 1992

Keen, Sam, and Anne Valley Fox. *Your Mythic Journey.* 2nd ed. Los Angeles: Jeremy Tarcher, 1989.

L'Engle, Madeleine. *The Rock That Is Higher: Story as Truth.* Wheaton, Ill.: Harold Shaw,1993.

―――. "Tell Me a Story." *Victoria,* April 1995, pp. 32-33.

Livo, Norma. "The Golden Spoon: Preserving Family History." *The National Storytelling Journal,* Summer 1984, pp. 8-10.

Livo, Norma, and Sandra A. Reitz. *Storytelling: Process and Practice.* Littleton, Colo.: Libraries Unlimited, 1986.

May, Rollo. *The Cry for Myth.* New York: W. W. Norton, 1991.

Miles, Midge. *Sacred Storytelling.* Kansas City, Mo.: Credence Cassettes, 1993.

Meltz, Barbara F. "Storytelling Holds More Than Fun." *Akron Beacon Journal,* May 14, 1992, p. C3.

Moore, Robin. *Awakening the Hidden Storyteller: How to Build a Storytelling Tradition in Your Family.* Boston: Shambhala, 1991.

National Storytelling Association. *Tales as Tools: The Power of Story in the Classroom.* Jonesborough, Tenn.: National Storytelling Press, 1994.

Oliver, Laura. "Comrades in Arms." *Country Living,* August 1995, p. 34.

Pellowski, Anne. *The Family Storytelling Handbook.* New York: Macmillan, 1987.

―――. *The World of Storytelling.* Bronx, N.Y.: H. W. Wilson, 1990.

Pipher, Mary. *The Shelter of Each Other: Rebuilding Our Families.* New York: G. P. Putnam, 1996.

Simpkinson, Charles, and Anne Simpkinson. *Sacred Stories: A Celebration of the Power of Stories to Transform and Heal.* San Francisco: Harper & Row, 1993.

Smith, Charles A. *From Wonder to Wisdom: Using Stories to Help Children Grow.* New York: New American Library, 1989.

Smith, Jimmy Neil. Introduction to *Homespun: Tales from America's Favorite Storytellers.* Edited by Jimmy Neil Smith. Jonesborough, Tenn./New York: Crown, 1988.

Solomon, Harvey. "Never Forget: Spielberg Gives Survivors Forum to Tell Chilling

Stories of the Holocaust." *Medina County Gazette,* December 27, 1995, p. 10.
Stone, Elizabeth. *Black Sheep and Kissing Cousins: How Our Family Stories Shape Us.* New York: Times Books, 1988.
Trousdale, Ann M., Sue A. Woestehoff and Marni Schwartz, eds. *Give a Listen: Stories of Storytelling in School.* Urbana, Ill.: National Council of Teachers of English, 1994.
Wallas, Lee. *Stories That Heal: Re-parenting Adult Children of Dysfunctional Families Using Hypnotic Stories in Psychotherapy.* New York: W. W. Norton, 1991.